DEMOCRACY CHALLENGED

ALSO BY WILLIAM HEWARD GRAFFTEY

The Senseless Sacrifice: A Black Paper on Medicine

Lessons from the Past

Why Canadians Get the Politicians and Governments They Don't Want

Portraits from a Life

DEMOCRACY
CHALLENGED

How to End One-Party Rule in Canada

William Heward Grafftey

Véhicule Press

MONTRÉAL

Published with the generous assistance of The Canada Council for the
Arts, the Book Publishing Industry Development Program of the
Department of Canadian Heritage, and the Société de développement
des entreprises culturelles du Québec (SODEC).

Cover design: David Drummond
Cover photo of author: Thomas Leon Königsthal, Jr.
Set in Adobe Minion by Simon Garamond
Printed by AGMV-Marquis Inc.

CATALOGUING IN PUBLICATION DATA

Grafftey, Heward, 1928-
Democracy challenged : how to end one-party rule in Canada

Includes index.
ISBN 1-55065-158-7

1. Progressive Conservative Party of Canada—History. 2. Canada—
Politics and government—20th century. 3. Progressive Conservative Party of
Canada. 4. Canada—Politics and government—1993- I. Title.

JL197.P7G727 2002   324.27104   C2002-902047-6

Published by Véhicule Press
P.O.B. 125, Place du Parc Station
Montréal, Québec H2X 4A3

www.vehiculepress.com

Printed in Canada on alkaline paper.

To Louis Cournoyer, the late Gaëtan Mireault,
the late Fabie Shaw, and the hundreds of party
workers—footsoldiers—without whom I would never have
been elected to the House of Commons seven times.

AN APPRECIATION

When it comes to thanking those who helped me with this book, it is hard to know where to begin. A sincere thanks to Dr. Luc Fortin at the University of Ottawa and Dr. Michael O'Neill of Hull. To Richard Paré, Parliamentary Librarian, and Gilles Marleau, Chief, Reference, my thanks for all your help. To John Metcalfe and Bruce Henry, thank you for your editorial acumen. To Nathalie Carrière, many thanks for preparing the manuscript. To Julien Hutchinson of Toronto, thank you for your insights and observations, especially as they touched upon matters of policy. Finally, to Simon Dardick, Nancy Marrelli, and Vicki Marcok, of Véhicule Press, a thousand thanks for taking on this project with me.

Contents

INTRODUCTION 11

CHAPTER ONE
The Diefenbaker Years 1956 – 1962 15

CHAPTER TWO
The Diefenbaker Years 1963 – 1967 45

CHAPTER THREE
The Stanfield Years 1967 – 1976 69

CHAPTER FOUR
Clark to Mulroney 82

CHAPTER FIVE
Mulroney, Campbell, Charest, and Clark Recycled 110

CHAPTER SIX
A Brief History of French Canada 124

CHAPTER SEVEN
A Short History of Western Canada 150

CHAPTER EIGHT
The Power of the Finance Department 166

CHAPTER NINE
Where To Now? 180

APPENDIX: CAMPAIGNING TO WIN 195
INDEX 199

There is a tide in the affairs of men,
Which, taken at the flood, leads on to fortune;
Omitted, all the voyage of their life
Is bound in shallows and in miseries.
On such a full sea are we now afloat;
And we must take the current when it serves,
Or lose our ventures.

—Shakespeare (*Julius Caesar*, IV, 3)

Introduction

Canadians are worried. They don't like one-party rule. They see a divided Opposition that handed power to the Liberals in the last two federal elections. Unless things change quickly, they sense that the next election will merely be another coronation for the Grits.

They see the once great Progressive Conservative Party reduced to twelve seats in the House, hived off in a corner of the Opposition benches.

All over the free world people are cynically turning their backs on politicians and traditional political parties. Canada is no exception. Voters feel our parties and elected representatives are letting them down; they are not addressing contemporary grassroots concerns.

Our elected government in Ottawa is satisfied with the status quo. Mr. Chrétien and his cast of supporting MPs feel they will automatically be re-elected. The Opposition remains completely silent on the big issues, like health care, facing Canada and our people. Seven years ago the World Health Organization cited our Medicare system as being number one in the world; now, in 2002, it is ranked thirty-ninth. The Government is out of touch with people's concerns about the environment, the plight of the Western farmer, and our falling dollar. As the dollar falls, so does our standard of living in comparison to other countries. The level of poverty, by any definition, is far too high in Canada. Most Canadians do not want to live in a country where the rich grow richer and the poor grow poorer. There is unrest among backbenchers of all parties. They need new and meaningful power as do parliamentary committees. The Government does nothing. Inexplicably, the Opposition remains silent.

Invariably, we get candidates, MPs, and leaders we don't want. Why? Most of the time, individual Canadians have no say in nominating them. This situation cries out for reform.

This book is written in the belief that Canadians want to return to a two-party system. We are ill-served when the ruling majority Liberals do not see a credible alternative on the Opposition benches. The Prime

Minister should look across the floor of the House into the eyes of the Leader of the Opposition and say to himself, "There is my possible replacement." The Bloc and the Alliance have divided the vote and given the Grits a free ride. This is ironic for the Liberals' energy policy of the 1980s stimulated Western alienation and led to the creation of the Reform Party, followed by the Alliance. Likewise the Liberal mishandling of Quebec nationalism aided and abetted the Bloc.

When I first ran for the Commons in 1957, the Liberals had been in power for twenty-two years. Many people quipped that Canada would be the only country to keep one party in power forever and still be called a democracy. I disagreed; it was time for a change. Today, many Canadians feel the way I did in 1957. In that year there was an opposition party that could take power. In 2002, matters are worse. The role of Her Majesty's Loyal Opposition fluctuates between two regional parties, neither of which has a hope of winning power.

Between 1956 and 2001, despite winning overwhelming majorities in 1958 and again in 1984, the Progressive Conservative Party fell from grace. In 1963, the Party handed power to the Liberals on a platter when John Diefenbaker unnecessarily let his government fall. Almost seventeen years later Joe Clark repeated Diefenbaker's error when he unnecessarily let his minority government collapse. This, in my view, was the single greatest poltical blunder in Canadian history.

My great-grandfather's youngest child and son was Frank P. Jones. He founded Canada Cement with Max Aitken, later to become Lord Beaverbrook. He was subsequently Prime Minister Robert Borden's Director of Munitions during World War I, a sort of unelected C.D. Howe. My great-uncle Frank once said "Experience is that marvellous thing that enables you to recognize a mistake when you make it again." Joe Clark did not learn from experience, and acted without consulting his cabinet colleagues.

Some weeks before he died, I had lunch with Pierre Elliott Trudeau. He told me, "I really liked Joe Clark."

"Hell, you should have," I replied, "he handed you back your power on a platter."

Trudeau smiled and added, "Joe went for an election because he thought he could win."

Despite the blunders, there were accomplishments. Diefenbaker humanized the party and put it in touch with the grass roots. No special interests interfered with his populist instincts. Labour Minister Michael Starr's Winter Works program aided municipalities, coast to coast, to employ workers during a slack period for employment. Minister of Agriculture Alvin Hamilton's Agricultural Rehabilitation and Development Act plan, put together with provincial cooperation, helped stimulate the economies of rural areas.

The Stanfield and Clark years were not remarkable for policy or program initiatives, but their civility, honesty and moderate policy positions enhanced the public's perception of federal politics. How often did I hear, "Stanfield was the best Prime Minister we never had." During the short-lived Clark government, I had the privilege, as Science Minister, to pilot the only significant initiative through cabinet—a five-year plan to assist research at Canadian universities. The plan was embraced enthusiastically by the science community and is still doing much good. Even Brian Mulroney's most severe critics give him and his government full marks for the Free Trade Agreement (NAFTA) and the goods and services tax (GST), which were, and are, good for the Canadian economy. During Jean Charest's short-lived term as leader of the party caucus, he played a significant role in the Quebec referendum.

Not long ago, I attended a reception at the home atop Westmount Mountain of Senator Leo Kolber, a fellow law student with me at McGill University years ago. Kolber has been a major fundraiser for the Liberal Party. At the reception, Jean Chrétien announced to all in hearing distance that I had won seven elections in Quebec, most of the time under nearly impossible conditions. He went on to say, "You know, Heward, I do my best, work very hard, and sleep like a kitten at night." "You should," I replied. "You have no serious opposition." Jean smiled and retorted. "Don't expect us to pull the Tory irons out of the fire!" How right he was.

With hard work and faith, the Progressive Conservative Party can, and will, form the next government; the election will not merely be yet another coronation of the Liberal Party. The Party must "earn" power. There is no use crying about one-party rule and blaming the Liberals for it. This situation has come about largely because of the weaknesses of the Progressive Conservative Party in leadership, organization, and fundraising.

The Party is in need of good constituency candidates and of well-articulated policies that it will stick with once in power. The challenge is great, for the Liberals are well-funded and have one of the best organized political machines in the Western world. How else could they be called, as the late Jack Pickersgill frequently reminded us, "the natural governing party"? We must be progressive in social policy and conservative in economic policy. Canadians want to be governed by dynamic moderates. Voters marginalize parties that swing too far to the left or right. The Progressive Conservative Party's policies must demonstrate to Canadians how we shall, once again, unite the country and eliminate alienation, especially in the West and Quebec.

CHAPTER ONE

The Diefenbaker Years 1956-1962

When John Diefenbaker was named leader of the Progresssive Conservative Party in 1956 he replaced George Drew who had resigned some months before, ostensibly because of ill health. Nobody gave "The Dief" much of a chance to unseat the Liberals and the popular Prime Minister, Louis St-Laurent. But most people underestimated the campaigning abilities of the man from Prince Albert, Saskatchewan. Diefenbaker had swallowed many defeats. Only after incredibly hard work was he elected to the House of Commons.

The infamous Pipeline Debate of 1957 paved the way for the Tories and their new leader. In order to ensure passage of legislation to create the pipeline, the Liberals imposed closure. The ensuing uproar made national headlines. Enraged Opposition members marched from their seats, gathering around the Speaker's chair, shouting and shaking their fists at him. Donald Fleming even draped the Canadian flag over his desk. The long debate highlighted Grit arrogance after twenty-two long years in power.

St-Laurent had just completed an around-the-world trip. He was tired and the Grits' lacklustre campaign showed it. After an incredibly vigorous and colourful campaign in the June 1957 election, Diefenbaker led his Party to a minority government. The Tories even went from four to eight seats in Quebec.

Soon after the 1957 vote, St-Laurent retired, to be replaced by Lester B. Pearson. He had been an outstanding foreign minister in the Liberal cabinet. However, Pearson's abilities as an Opposition leader would prove to be less than outstanding.

In March 1958, Diefenbaker went to the Governor General and called an election for the following June. "Follow John" was his slogan and Canadians chose to do so, giving the Tories a massive majority of

205 seats, and reducing the once-mighty Grits to a corporal's guard of 50 seats.

Many thought that the Progressive Conservatives, with such a majority, would hold on to power for an eternity. After the 1958 election, as I was standing in line outside the Clerk's office ready to be sworn in, Paul Martin, Sr. stood beside me. He said, "How lucky you are to be entering the House at a young age, when your Party will be in power for a very long time." But four years later Martin would be a major factor in bringing the new government down.

The election was a catastrophe for the Party. Diefenbaker was more comfortable in opposition than in government. He could neither understand nor perform well in the new television age. He was not a team player. He was a loner who could not get on with, encourage, or organize people. The Dief, while a formidable campaigner, was disorganized. He became manipulative in office and lost the trust and confidence of colleagues he should have been able to count on. As incredible as it may sound, I don't think he really wanted to be prime minister. He relished the role of the underdog, fighting the mythical establishment which he often referred to as "they."

While dining at my home in my riding, Dief once told me that winning more cases before the Supreme Court than any other Canadian lawyer had been a greater honour for him than being prime minister. I didn't believe him. He told me that when he was a small boy in Saskatoon, he could not afford a ticket for a baseball game and installed himself behind a wooden fence in the outfield. He put his eye to a knothole to see the game. A security guard caught him and kicked him in the pants. The result was a black eye. John always felt that established authority was kicking him and giving him a black eye, and he vigorously challenged it. Such an attitude would hamper his ability to govern.

The Government was severely wounded between 1958 and 1962 by the cancellation of the production of the Avro-Arrow aircraft, Finance Minister Donald Fleming's continual fighting with the Governor of the Bank of Canada and the provinces, and the devaluation of the Canadian dollar during the 1962 election. Like Diefenbaker, Fleming was happier in opposition than in government and preferred a fight in the House to governing.

Justice Minister Davie Fulton's inept handling of Joey Smallwood during the Newfoundland Loggers' Strike severely wounded the government and damaged the Party in Newfoundland. The Tories clashed with Premier Bill Bennett of British Columbia over the Columbia River Treaty with the United States. The *coup de grace* was the Bomarc Missile Crisis that pitted Foreign Affairs Minister Howard Green against the indomitable Defence Minister, Doug Harkness. The issue defeated, in 1963, the minority government elected in 1962.

There was also bad luck. The Party's Quebec base was seriously diminished by the sudden death of Premier Duplessis of Quebec on September 7, 1959, and the subsequent deaths of successive Union Nationale leaders. Paul Sauvé died suddenly less than four months after succeeding Duplessis. Daniel Johnson miraculously led Duplessis's old Union Nationale party back to power in the late sixties, but he, too, died suddenly in office.

Leadership

The process of leadership selection for the major Canadian political parties goes back to Confederation. In 1867, the Governor General played a major role in selecting the leader of the ruling majority party. Later, the cabinet would approve the naming of a new chief upon the retirement of the incumbent leader. The next step involved the whole elected parliamentary caucus. When Laurier retired as head of the Liberal Party, at the urging of influential members of the editorial board of the *Globe and Mail* in Toronto, he advocated a party convention, including all rank and file party members as delegates, to choose his successor. Mackenzie King was the first party leader to be selected by the kind of convention we know. But party conventions soon became elitist. The grassroots had little say in the process. Conventions have also become corrupted with the busing in of voters who are often not even party members, to choose a candidate. Because the grass roots are ignored, the party elite has given us unelectable leaders whom we did not want.

In December 1956, John Diefenbaker was chosen as the leader of the Progressive Conservative Party. I attended the convention and witnessed the proceedings. Not only my Party, but all parties were guilty of what I experienced in Ottawa. The grass roots were ignored. The organization of the delegate selection process was in virtual disarray. For one thing, only those who could afford the trip to the Nation's Capital got to vote.

When a constituency did not have the necessary five delegates to vote in Ottawa, "blow-in" delegates were substituted to fill the vacancies. For example, only two delegates from my constituency of Brome-Missisquoi were in Ottawa to vote. We could not afford the travel and hotel costs. The three vacant delegate spots were subsequently filled by blow-ins from other parts of Canada. In the case of Brome-Missisquoi, one blow-in came from Montreal and the other two from Toronto and Vancouver. Thus was John Diefenbaker named leader.

By the mid-1990s, enough was enough and the "one member-one vote" process was adopted by the Progressive Conservative and Alliance parties. Joe Clark and Stockwell Day were selected by all members of their parties.

The Quebec Scene

After Diefenbaker's victory at the polls in June 1957, the subsequent minority parliament was most productive. John A. Macdonald had often said, "Give me good wood and I shall build a strong cabinet." Diefenbaker thought he had little or no good wood to deal with from Quebec. This seemed to persist even after Diefenbaker gained a huge majority after the 1958 elections with over fifty members from Quebec. At any rate, the chemistry between Léon Balcer and Diefenbaker was bad. The former threatened to boycott the 1956 Party convention because Diefenbaker refused to have his nomination either proposed or seconded by a Francophone. The French press were forever on the new leader's back for his thin Quebec cabinet representation.

While my riding is just a forty-minute drive from Montreal, it could have been a thousand miles away as far as city journalists and the Party establishment were concerned. The Conservative Party hierarchy in

Montreal had to be seen to be believed. They had never really accepted Dief and he knew it. Dief was always fighting the Tory brass, but he was also overawed by them. Once he became prime minister he made little effort to bury the hatchet with the party bigwigs. I always felt that Dief could have handled the recalcitrant party establishment better, but it was perhaps too much to ask of a man who loved to play the underdog. After their two decades in the wilderness, the Tories seemed uneasy in power. Even as 1959 drew to a close, you could sense the suicidal instincts of our members; they would rather fight each other than the Grits. This was a Tory tradition. After Sir John A. Macdonald's death in 1891, Tory infighting became habitual. In short order, the party went through four leaders and prime ministers before Laurier and the Liberals took power in the land.

The Civil Service 1958 to 1963

Tommy Douglas once said of Diefenbaker, "John can smell a vote a hundred miles away, but he can't administer a peanut stand." While Douglas' observation is somewhat exaggerated, there is some truth in it. To direct a winning election campaign requires different skills and techniques from those talents required to run a good government. The people employed in a successful election campaign are not necessarily endowed with the talent to advise a prime minister and his cabinet. Diefenbaker and his ministers brought their old political associates to Ottawa to work as their assistants. They started off with the best of intentions, but they lost the battle they were supposed to have won. These assistants were snowed by the bureaucracy. It took no time for them to be coopted by the "civil service point of view." Even their ministers invariably became the prisoners of bureaucrats. There is really only one solution to this problem. Governments must come to power with a precise and well-defined policy agenda. Ministerial assistants and officials in the prime minister's office must ascertain that these policies are implemented with dispatch and loyalty. To humanize the bureaucracy and to make it responsive to government and public demands and realities constitutes a primary challenge for any new government. Diefenbaker and his ministers, often through no fault of their own, failed to meet this basic challenge.

Jack Pickersgill, an ex-senior civil servant, proclaimed that governments other than Grit are short-term aberrations that happen on rare occasions before the Canadian people turn quickly back to the Liberals. He was subconsciously expressing a point of view espoused by many senior bureaucrats. During the Grits' reign between 1935 and 1957, bureaucrats identified themselves with the Liberals, feeling they were the natural governing party that would be in power forever.

A number of events involving the Department of Finance had serious political repercussions during Diefenbaker's second Parliament. Finance Minister Don Fleming had been a formidable opposition member, hard-working, well-briefed, and ready to do political battle at the drop of a hat. Political confrontation was his forte, as he had shown when he led the Tory troops during the famous pipeline debate. As finance minister, his instinct for the political jugular soon became apparent when perhaps a little diplomacy and soft talk would have expedited his measures through Parliament. Doug Abbott, St-Laurent's able finance minister, used to charm the House, and his humour invariably saved the day for him and the Government when difficult and contentious issues were before the Commons. Not so for Fleming. His first major confrontation took place early in the 1958 Parliament and the lesson was that you should never take on a provincial premier unless your political ground is secure: the premier is normally closer to the voters. The issue concerned Ottawa's obligations to Newfoundland, the country's newest province. The disagreement over Term 29 caused half the Conservatives in the Newfoundland Assembly to bolt the Party and form one of their own. It also gave rise to a snap provincial election that showed Canada that Newfoundland felt that the federal government had failed to live up to its obligations. Smallwood gained a resounding victory at the polls.

Newfoundland and Term 29

Representatives of Newfoundland met in Quebec for constitutional talks as early as 1864. Although provisions had been made in the British North

America Act of 1867 for Newfoundland to enter Canada, union was rejected decisively in the 1869 Newfoundland election. In 1895, Newfoundland again considered the possibility, but financial issues proved insoluble and negotiations foundered. In 1946, a confederation movement again got underway and the next year a delegation arrived in Ottawa to "ascertain federal union." The King government's need to have a complete and comprehensive exchange of information led to the formation of ten subcommittees. (Joey Smallwood was a member of each!)

After the deliberations, Ottawa adopted a basis for union that was sent to Newfoundland. The terms of the union were approved by the Newfoundland legislature on February 18, 1949. Term 29 referred to a royal commission to recommend financial assistance for Newfoundland, if it was needed:

> In view of the difficulty of predicting with sufficient accuracy the financial consequences to Newfoundland of becoming a province of Canada, the government of Canada will appoint a royal commission within eight years from the date of union to review the financial position of the Province of Newfoundland and to recommend the form and scale of additional financial assistance, if any, that may be required to continue public services at the levels and standards reached subsequent to the date of Union, without resorting to taxation more burdensome, having regard to capacity to pay, than that obtaining generally in the region compromising the Maritime provinces of Nova Scotia, New Brunswick and Prince Edward Island.

From 1949 to 1962, Ottawa contributed eight million dollars to the Newfoundland government. The catch was the preamble to the federal bill covering financial assistance to the province. It stated that the situation would be reviewed in 1962, and disregarded the notion of payments in perpetuity. The political fallout was predictable: Smallwood hammered away at Ottawa's stinginess. I suspected that the federal department of Finance and its officials were isolated from the political debate between Ottawa and St. John's. Smallwood was not easy to deal with, but even in our caucus, a number of Newfoundland members and their families had voted against Confederation. Indeed, on the day following the vote for Confederation, many Newfoundlanders had draped their homes in black. The Term 29 debate was full of political danger for Ottawa and eventually hurt the Diefenbaker government.

The Coyne Affair

Open warfare broke out between the governor of the Bank of Canada, James Coyne, and the Diefenbaker government late in 1960 and the following spring. To most members of the Conservative caucus, James Coyne was a closet Liberal. The governor, in a series of speeches, had publicly attacked the government for its alleged fiscal irresponsibility. In December 1959 news report he told the Investment Dealer's Association in Toronto:

> No economy as advanced as ours should allow itself to be moulded into a pattern of employment which is dependent for any extended period on capital expenditures financed by foreign money-borrowing on such a scale.

By October 1960 Coyne's statements had become notably stronger. Speaking to the annual meeting of the Canadian Chamber of Commerce in Calgary, he said:

> We cannot expect to go on indefinitely buying goods and services from abroad in amounts greatly in excess of our exports, that is, buying on credit on a scale which requires large further increases in our foreign debt.
>
> We must, therefore, face the prospect of suffering at some stage a major restriction in the supply of goods

and services available for consumption and for expansion of capital facilities in Canada—or else we must set about providing for ourselves an amount of goods and services made in Canada through the employment of Canadians, in replacement of the supply from outside, upon which we have been so heavily dependent for the past decade.

In my view our present unemployment cannot be cured by blunderbuss methods of overall larger-scale monetary expansion and deficit finance.

The debate raged. Coyne charged the government with interference in monetary policy. Coyne's resignation was demanded on May 30, 1961, and in a letter to Fleming dated June 9 (and recorded in Hansard), Coyne stated:

One reason you gave why the government would not approve my reappointment was that the statements in public speeches I have made turned out to be embarrassing to the government and were being used by their opponents in Parliament and elsewhere for political purposes. You first spoke to me about this matter on March 18th last, and I have not made any public speeches since.

Coyne had more to say about his removal by the Diefenbaker government:

The sudden and unexplained demand for my resignation on May 30, the appearance of haste and urgency, and the blackmailing tactics used, suggested the present government had a plan to call a snap election, without a budget, or perhaps immediately after the budget speech was made, and subvert to the Bank of Canada under a new governor of their own choosing to assist them in financing expenditures and programs not authorized by Parliament.

Don Fleming's riposte was that the governor had interfered in the government's fiscal policy. The minister addressed the situation in the House on June 26, 1961:

> Until the autumn of 1959, the governor had not made a practice of making public speeches, but at that time he began to do so. For the next year and a half he made them with increasing force, frequency and fervour. Never was I or any other member of government consulted at any time in any respect whatever in regard to the making of those speeches or their contents.
>
> They quickly attracted public attention, which increased with each of those public utterances, principally because they were devoted almost entirely to fiscal, not monetary policy and thus entered upon one of those most controversial subjects in the whole world spectrum. The governor did not directly attack the Government, but it was not long before the government was bearing the full weight of his criticisms and strictures.
>
> He contended time and time again with ever increasing vehemence that the country was suffering from wrong fiscal policies and the absence of needed fiscal programs. Such, under our constitutional system, Mr. Speaker, are the responsibilities of the government, not the responsibilities of the Bank of Canada.

A second, and more direct, complaint against Coyne was introduced by Fleming on June 26:

> In the winter of 1957–58 I conveyed to him a request

for an easing of the requirements respecting the liquidity reserves of chartered banks. That request, which was designed by the Government to ease tight money, was rejected by the governor firmly and angrily.

The second move by which the Diefenbaker government sought to declare Coyne's post vacant was Bill C-114. The Opposition asked for a joint committee to hear both sides of the question. Their argument was that only Parliament could fire Coyne. The debate took an ugly turn when Coyne's pension rights were discussed.

Bill C-114 passed and Coyne was out, but by the time Louis Raminsky was appointed governor on July 24, 1961, both the government and the Bank of Canada had been hurt. The political infighting created public cynicism and lost Canada prestige abroad. In *Canadian Business* (September 1996), William Thomas captures the essence of the Coyne Affair:

> To many Canadians it was a national embarrassment. Canada—with its solid-as-a-rock banking system, with a former governor of its central bank whom foreign governments seek out for advice and help on national banking problems, a country which American editorial writers frequently hold up to their government as one which follows the path of fiscal and monetary rectitude—has shown to the world a less-than-solid grip on a vital aspect of national administration.

Skeletons in the Cupboard

Diefenbaker was an amazing individual—complicated, eccentric and, in many ways, larger than life. Unfortunately he was his own worst enemy and, in a peculiar manner, alienated those who normally would have remained loyal to him.

Like many prime ministers with large majorities, he was faced with the unwelcome challenge of keeping his restless backbenchers happy. Prime ministers' tremendous power, together with the intrusive role of the bureaucracy, tends to make rubber stamps of backbenchers, many of whom had enviable records of "getting things done" back home. Soon after Parliament got under way in 1958, I was appointed to a seat on the estimates committee, examining current budgetary estimates. We sat throughout the summer months, often on Saturday mornings, under the able chairmanship of Arthur Smith, the member for Calgary South. Ottawa gets extremely humid in the summer. There was no air conditioning in the Centre Block, and we were working in a virtual steam bath. The committee first examined the estimates of the Department of National Defence. When I asked why the estimated cost of a frigate had doubled by the time it was finally launched, an irritated admiral questioned my sense of patriotism. Our report was made and submitted to Defence Minister George Pearkes, but ministers are not obliged to accept such recommendations and they were largely ignored by Pearkes and his officials.

Unlike their counterparts in Washington, our parliamentary committees are toothless forums without adequate research back-up and expertise. When I testified with Ralph Nader on the question of car safety before the Senate Commerce Committee of Congress in the late winter of 1966, it was easy to see that there had been a great deal of expert research available to the committee. It had real power and was taken seriously.

In Canada, the recommendations of parliamentary committees are usually shelved and ignored by ministers and their staff. Some members skilfully use the committees as publicity forums to influence public opinion, but this tends to be the exception. I found it hard to take committee work seriously under the prevailing handicaps and circumstances. Members were stuck into parliamentary committees to keep them busy and out of the hair of the bureaucrats and the ministers who were running the show. The voice of the people is rarely heard. Today, backbenchers are becoming increasingly restless as Jean Chrétien has tightened his grip.

Diefenbaker employed manipulative tactics to soothe the nerves of his restless backbenchers—tactics which compromised his veracity and, eventually, his ability to lead. Some said he was forgetful, but he knew exactly what he was doing.

My colleague, the member for Charlevoix, now Senator Martial Asselin, was a case in point. Diefenbaker once called Asselin back from the United Nations, where he was a delegate, to inform him that he wished to appoint him as parliamentary secretary to the minister of external affairs. By the time Asselin had arrived in Ottawa, Diefenbaker had changed his mind. Just before the 1963 election, Diefenbaker called Asselin to his office once again. Asselin, a protégé of Léon Balcer, had been defeated in the 1962 election, and was campaigning hard for re-election. Diefenbaker informed Asselin that he intended to appoint him to the cabinet as minister of forestry within the coming week. Since Asselin was no longer a member of parliament, and had to work hard for re-election in Charlevoix, he asked Dief to postpone the appointment till after the election. Dief refused and asked Asselin to report for his swearing-in the following week. However, when Asselin showed up at the Prime Minister's office in Ottawa some days later, nobody had even heard of his proposed nomination, and Diefenbaker denied ever having made the offer of a cabinet position. At the next cabinet meeting, Balcer confronted Diefenbaker, threatening to leave the cabinet unless the promise to Asselin was kept. Balcer then dismissed himself from the cabinet room and went downtown where he watched two consecutive movies until late in the afternoon. He returned to Parliament Hill to find his cabinet colleagues and members of the press corps crowded into his waiting room. His colleagues notified him that an emergency cabinet meeting had been called. Pierre Sévigny, George Hees, and Don Fleming had all announced their intention to quit the 1963 minority government. Unable to face the escalation of this mass ministerial defection, Diefenbaker backed down, and Asselin was sworn in at Rideau Hall soon after.

Dief made promises of appointments to cabinet, parliamentary secretaryships, and other positions to scores of members without any intention of carrying them out. The results were disastrous.

In spite of Dief's obvious drawbacks, I supported him in that he was preferable to the elitist alternative which had held our party captive in the past and could do so once more.

Diefenbaker was a House of Commons man and a populist at heart. Even in Quebec, he did everything possible to make sure that nomination meetings were openly and democratically held. In a letter addressed to me just after the first session of the 1958 Parliament, Diefenbaker wrote:

> As a party, we have much to be proud of, but we must, at all costs, guard against over-confidence, particularly in the matter of constituency organization. In many parts of the country, the organizations which carried us through the elections of 1957 and 1958 are comparatively new and much remains to be done in consolidating the ground gained. I have asked our National Headquarters to undertake (in cooperation with our members, constituency presidents, and former candidates) a complete check of the status of the organization in all 265 constituencies. The objective for the period between now and the opening of the next session is the establishment of a broadly based, representative Federal Conservative Association in every constituency in Canada. By this I mean an association which will 1) invite into its membership all who may wish to associate themselves with the future of the Party; 2) have an up-to-date written constitution; 3) have a fully elected executive; 4) hold regular meetings of both the executive and the association.

As the parliamentary session drew to a close in mid-July of 1959, it was evident that John Diefenbaker had changed the face of the old Tory party. Its previous Bay Street and exclusively WASP image gave way to a party that was more populist. People from many walks of life and diverse ethnic backgrounds now felt at home in a party that occupied the middle of the road, a position the Liberals had maintained with such devastating success for so many years. An editorial comment, typical at that time, appeared in the *Sherbrooke Daily Record* of July 21, 1959. It cited the fact that, after a year of majority government, party patterns were still confused; the very size of the parliamentary majority "posed a problem of party management for the Conservatives." The editorial continued:

> The prime minister attracted the majority of new young voters and while the right wing of the Conservative party remains, it has no choice but to put itself under moderate, or even mildly radical, leadership.
>
> The Liberals have not only lost their comfortable middle-of-the-road spot to the Conservatives, they have been stripped of all but a handful of their leaders. The majority of the old Liberal cabinet have quit politics for business and it will take some time to build up a new "shadow cabinet" competent enough to offer itself to the voters as an alternative government.
>
> The outnumbered opposition MPs have managed to kick up enough disturbance to make the last session of Parliament interesting, but they are flailing out in all directions. Sometime before the next election, the Liberals will have to decide whether they are going to take over the right wing—and hope to gather some support from right-wing Conservatives, squeeze out of the CCF on the left (and thus lose their own right-wingers), or try to push back into the middle now occupied by Mr. Diefenbaker's Conservatives.

Diefenbaker's stress on grass roots organization for the his party was undone by Stanfield, Clark, and Mulroney. These leaders worked from the top downwards and, once more, the Party, besides losing most of its seats in the House of Commons, has become an elitist conclave with no real organization at the constituency level. Our party foot soldiers have disappeared and only a major party membership drive can begin to rectify this situation.

During the 1958 majority Parliament other specific incidents did harm to Diefenbaker and his government.

The Avro Arrow

On February 20, 1959, a day that is still referred to as Black Friday in the Canadian aircraft industry, Diefenbaker rose in the Commons to cancel the Avro Arrow, the CF-105 fighter/interceptor which experts maintain could still be one of the best aircraft in the world. The prime minister claimed that the plane would soon be obsolete and that a general had told him it could not even get back home when it had reached its targeted destination. He believed that the day of the manned bomber was over. Instead, he opted for the Bomarc missile, then later even tried to get rid of it, a move that eventually helped speed our defeat and led to another prolonged period in opposition.

The Avro was developed by A. V. Roe Canada Ltd., established in 1945 as a subsidiary of the British Hawker Siddeley Group, at a time when the Canadian government was concerned over the fate of our gigantic wartime aircraft industry. It had employed a hundred and sixteen thousand workers in 1944. It had built more than sixteen thousand planes during the war. Avro's first fighter, the CF-100 Canuck, was a straight-wing conventional plane. Its successor, the Arrow, was to be a much more complex aircraft.

The Liberals were quick to point out that, with the cancellation of the Arrow, twenty-two thousand Canadians would be thrown out of work, most of them at the A.V. Roe and Orenda engine plants in Toronto. The rest were mostly suppliers from Montreal. An estimated four hundred and seventy-five million dollars in development and production costs already spent was wasted. The closure led to the emigration of the best of our aerospace talent. Arrow's chief aerodynamist James Chamberlain became project manager for the Gemini space program. Every major American aerospace program, from the Boeing 747 to the moon shots to the F-14, had Arrow veterans in key positions. When Diefenbaker ordered that all the planes be scrapped, he crippled our hard-won technological base in the aircraft industry and impaired the future of high technology in Canada.

One factor that contributed to the eventual doom of the Arrow was the bad behaviour displayed by the industry's senior executive, Crawdon Gordon. He swore a lot in Diefenbaker's office and shocked the latter's Baptist sensitivities. Another factor was that briefings from the then Department of Defence Production were flawed and inadequate, allowing too much scope for Dief's impulsive decision-making.

Whatever the justification of Diefenbaker's announcement in the Commons, the political handling of the question was horrendously inept. To scrap the planes that had already been built was a colossal error. Great damage was done and the political fallout continued to the next election and beyond.

The Loggers' Strike

That same winter of 1959 another crisis faced the Government—the Newfoundland logger's strike. For twenty-five years the loggers had been represented by local unions in the Newfoundland Loggers' Association. These unions had effected some improvements, but living and working conditions were generally poor and, in contrast to the most modern mainland camps, primitive. The work week was sixty hours and the basic rate of pay was one dollar and five cents per hour. Bunkhouses were dingy, poorly heated, and inadequately ventilated. The loggers's diet was monotonous and rather unhealthy. Staple foods were salt beef, potatoes, carrots, turnips, and cabbage. Breakfast consisted of beans and bad bologna.

In 1956, the loggers had invited the International Woodworkers of America (IWA) to Newfoundland. The IWA was denounced as radical and violent, but it had the support of the workers. They began their strike on December 31, 1958 for better wages and living conditions in the camps.

The striking workers set up picket lines at roads leading to the logging camps. Reports said that violence had broken out and that strike-breakers and their families had been threatened and hurt. Premier Joey Smallwood called in the Newfoundland police and the RCMP to keep peace. On March 10 a violent battle broke out at Badger between hundreds of striking loggers and the RCMP (supported by the Newfoundland constabulary) as the company was taking more men into the camps. One policeman died and another was seriously injured, as were two of the strikers. Newfoundland asked Ottawa to send in more RCMP, but Diefenbaker refused. RCMP Commissioner Leonard H. Nicholson, who had been the head of the Mounties for nearly eight years, resigned in protest over what he called the Government's "reprehensible" action.

Joey Smallwood decided that the IWA would have to go because it had precipitated violence, was disrupting the province's economy, and could cause financial ruin by closing down the Anglo-Newfoundland Development Company. The methods the premier employed to realize his aim were disgraceful. His most remarkable manoeuvre was to claim that there were links between the IWA in Newfoundland and the International Brotherhood of Teamsters in the United States. Smallwood described the Teamsters as "pimps, panderers, white slavers, murderers, embezzlers, extortioners, manslaughterers, dope peddlers." Early in March the Newfoundland legislature gave third reading to a bill that would allow the lieutenant-governor-in-council, under certain conditions, "to dissolve any union in the province.." The IWA was de-certified as a bargaining agent for the loggers.

About a week before the legislation came into force, the premier undertook to form his own union to represent the loggers—the Newfoundland Brotherhood of Wood Workers. Smallwood appointed Max Lane, a Liberal member of the Newfoundland legislature, to head the new union. Oddly, Lane was also the dominant figure in the Newfoundland Federation of Fisherman, a semi-political go-between for provincial fishermen and the government. The loggers promptly dubbed Smallwood's new union the "fish and chip" union.

The Anglo-Newfoundland Development Company had not been idle. It had been rushing workers into the camps by back roads from wherever they could find them. Union pickets patrolled the company's main camps and were especially in evidence in the small logging community of Badger.

With the IWA certification lifted under the legislation, and the union's members barred from picketing under penalty of heavy fines and jail, the Smallwood-sponsored rival loggers' union made an agreement with the Anglo-Newfoundland Development Company on March 13.

Federal Opposition leader Mike Pearson called for an inquiry into the strike, but Davie Fulton, the Minister of Justice, stated that the Mounties had carried out their duties with fairness and efficiency. He saw no necessity for setting up a judicial inquiry. Newfoundlanders, facing their gravest problem since Confederation, felt that the rest of Canada was showing a frustrating lack of understanding.

In private conversations, Diefenbaker let it be known that he would not allow his government to be associated with anything like the 1919 Winnipeg strike, where the RCMP had been used as strike breakers. Whatever Fulton's feelings were in the matter, the prime minister's views carried the day. Since the 1956 convention, the two men had been uneasy with one another, and the handling of the logger's strike only made things worse.

Smallwood milked the crisis for all he could get. I fully supported the federal government's decision not to send in more RCMP reinforcements.

The Columbia River Treaty

It was also during this winter session that debate commenced on a proposed development that would compare in importance with the St. Lawrence Seaway. Many years of wrangling with the United States concerning a power development on the Columbia River had not produced any results. But early in 1959, Washington agreed to the suggestion that an International Joint Commission be given the task of working out the details of an agreement between the two governments. The agreement would provide for the payment for downstream benefits arising out of power development on the river. Ottawa and the British Columbia government had cooperated, although subsequently the provincial government in BC did not see eye to eye with Ottawa. The basic fact was that Canada should get back power produced in the United States as downstream benefits for the storage of water upstream north of the border. Ottawa was attempting to create a national energy board that would be able to give leadership and direction in the handling of these sources of energy.

The Columbia River Treaty was signed by Diefenbaker and Eisenhower in Washington on January 17, 1961.

General McNaughton, the chairman of the International Joint Commission, condemned certain aspects of the proposed treaty for giving away Canadian control of the whole river basin. This matter proved to be a thorn in the side for Diefenbaker. It brought him and his ministers into conflict with BC Premier W.A.C. Bennett, and the party's support in British Columbia suffered greatly. Doing battle with Bennett and with Joey Smallwood got great press, but Ottawa lost the political battles and eventually seats in both provinces. The lesson here is not to take on political battles with the provinces—they win every time.

The Winds of Change

The winds of change were blowing. Ottawa-Quebec relations were difficult after the death, in 1959, of Quebec's premier Maurice Duplessis. Then there was the sudden death of his successor, Paul Sauvé, and the spring election of Jean Lesage's Liberals. John F. Kennedy was elected to the White House, replacing Dwight Eisenhower, with whom the prime minister had enjoyed a relatively easy and cordial association. Relations with the United States were soon to sour.

While I do not accept the notion that 1960 constituted a magic date in Quebec, inaugurating the Quiet Revolution and our emergence from the dark ages, nevertheless religious, social, and economic attitudes were changing quickly in the province. I never understood how a revolution could be quiet. When the pundits analyse the Quiet Revolution I am reminded of the observations of Felipe Fernández-Armesto in his book, *Millennium: A History of the Last Thousand Years*— "Scholars always think that every generation likes to spotlight its own modernity against the darkness of the past."

Any politician who failed to take account of the changes occurring in Quebec was courting disaster. The secularization of Quebec's educational institutions in the early 1960s, the declining influence of the clergy in secular matters, the rise of a well-educated francophone entrepreneurial group, and a dramatic drop in the birth rate were just a few of the forces then at work.

I did not recognize it at the time, but Réal Caouette and his Créditistes were getting up a head of steam and precipitating even more changes in Quebec politics, changes that had not been foreseen by the authorities in Ottawa. Caouette attacked the "two old parties" with the force of a zealot. His humour and old-style oratory were featured on Saturday night TV after the wrestling matches, and appealed to small town and rural Quebec; the Liberals and the Tories were equal targets.

The winds of populism and extreme nationalism were blowing simultaneously. Continued poverty in rural Quebec meant that many people expected little of the old-line parties. Caouette jumped into the void like a faith-healer, urging the populace to vote for the Créditistes, crying again and again, "You have nothing to lose!"

Although Diefenbaker referred only to Canadians and never, for example, to German-Canadians or Polish-Canadians, his unhyphenated Canadianism was suspect for francophones. He was rightfully proud of being our first prime minister of neither anglophone and nor francophone ancestry. He related this pride to the author Hugh MacLennan during an interview at Sussex Drive when he stressed his "One Canada" theme. Later, during a press interview after a speech in Hamilton, I volunteered that the "One Canada" theme, while laudable, was difficult for many francophones, who felt that it could, if carried to extremes, submerge the French fact in Canada into a general melting pot. On my return to Ottawa, I was called into Diefenbaker's office for a dressing down. When I tried to reply, he had already opened the door to encourage my hasty exit. Mike Starr was in the waiting room. He had heard the commotion and wondered whether or not he should enter the room and intervene.

The prime minister's relations with the press were beginning to deteriorate. Jim Nelson, his press secretary, seemed ill at ease in the job. There were no regular press conferences, but unlike St. Laurent, who studiously avoided the press, Diefenbaker was only too happy to talk to journalists. He was easy prey for their badgering as he entered and left the cabinet room. His performances during these scrums contributed as much as anything to the public view that the Government was wishy-washy and indecisive.

Jack Pickersgill, Paul Martin, Lionel Chevrier, and, later on, Judy LaMarsh, were outstanding in opposition. I called them the four horsemen. Almost alone, they kept the Government at bay. The federal Liberals were becoming more forceful and organized in opposition. Morale in our caucus was low. The prime minister held one interminable cabinet session after another. Indecision was the hallmark of these cabinet meetings and there was marked dissension amongst the ministers. Diefenbaker's tempestuous outbursts grew more frequent.

A subtle but formidable influence after 1960 was television. It changed the face of North American politics. John Diefenbaker was uncomfortable with the imperatives of Marshall McLuhan's "cool" medium. The jowel-shaking and gesticulating that served him well on the political platform, let him down badly on television.

Soon after the budget in 1960, Diefenbaker asked me to accompany him to a service club luncheon. Afterwards we were walking back to Parliament Hill when one of his aides mentioned a recent Gallup poll that showed our party still high in the national standings. Dief looked pensive, then quipped, "Don't forget that every politician has his Good Friday." Hearing him I had a strange feeling that he was listening to some prophetic inner voice; that, even with the biggest electoral majority in our history, he felt destined for a political crucifixion. Did he know how imminent it was? Had he subconsciously grown tired of governing after the relative freedom of the opposition years? Maybe an insatiable martyr complex had to be fed.

Perhaps no other event in 1960 signalled the passing of the older political generation more than the November election of forty-three year-old John Fitzgerald Kennedy to the presidency of the United States. From the launching of his campaign at Candlestick Park in San Francisco, after a series of compelling and exciting primary elections, through the campaign itself, with its televised debates and his confrontation with the Protestant clergy, suspicious that a Roman Catholic president could not uphold the Constitution in case of a crisis of conscience with the Vatican, Kennedy seemed to usher in a new political era. While Diefenbaker identified with Eisenhower, the communication barrier with the future occupant of the Oval Office made constructive dialogue too much to expect. The dreams of Camelot were not for Dief, and relations with the younger Kennedy would soon become a nightmare.

In the first half of 1961, Diefenbaker and Kennedy exchanged visits. In retrospect, we know that the seeds of ill will were sown between the two men during these exchanges. I found it hard to understand Dief's animosity towards Kennedy. He would derisively imitate the president's Boston drawl to me and quip, "When I say Canada must jump, Canada must jump!" No doubt Dief was conscious of the generation gap because he used to say, "I have no lessons to learn from that young whipper-snapper." Was it a case of reverse snobbery, as Dief sensed the moneyed power and influence of the Kennedys? Eleanor Roosevelt often referred to the reverse snobbery of Al Smith, the one-time governor of New York and Democratic nominee for the presidency in 1928—a self-made man who was patronizing towards her husband Franklin; Smith saw him as a prince of privilege from the banks of the Hudson, who had not come up the hard way as he had. Whatever the reason for Diefenbaker's dislike of Kennedy, things went from bad to worse. During his Ottawa visit in May, the president inadvertently dropped a note on the floor of the prime minister's office. It was subsequently brought to Dief's attention. "How do I deal with this SOB?" were the words Kennedy had scrawled to an aide.

The Liberals' policy conference in Kingston in September 1960 had turned out to be a landmark meeting. Pearson recognized that an era had come to an end and told the conference that the Liberal Party had used up its political inheritance and needed new ideas and new solutions for the nation's problems. He said, "A Liberal should always be the first to welcome the challenge of new ideas and first to move away from those that may have served their usefulness." Among the problems for which he said the party must find solutions were unemployment, the reduction of trade barriers, and the conversion of the European free trade area and the diminution of Canadian dependence on the U.S. market for trade and on American capital for development. Official Canadian policy, he said, had not changed with the advent of intercontinental missiles, nor was Canada as a world middle power making the contribution through its defence effort or its foreign policies that it could and should make to the preservation of world peace.

Maurice Lamontagne, Pearson's chief economic adviser, played a major role during and after the conference, as did Tom Kerr, the former editor of the *Winnipeg Free Press*. At Kingston, Walter Gordon honed his opposition to the official Liberal party line on free trade.

The major initiative at Kingston was the Liberal party's renunciation of nuclear weapons for the armed forces, a position Pearson had put forward forcibly during the last session of Parliament. Other innovations included universal medicare, a minimum wage, old-age pensions, and redistributive measures to provide social dividends for Canadian citizens.

While Diefenbaker had the right instincts, he let the Liberals act on the unfulfilled post-war national agenda. While it was not evident to the Conservative caucus at the time, in retrospect this period marked the beginning of the end for the Diefenbaker government. Defence and foreign policy, the deterioration of Canadian-U.S. relations, together with the public rift between Kennedy and Diefenbaker over defence matters, the Coyne Affair, federal-provincial relations, especially as they concerned Quebec under Lesage's new leadership—all spelled trouble for the prime minister, whose moods became increasingly unpredictable. There was only a tenuous unity in caucus. He had little understanding of, or confidence in, its membership, and from time to time, he would ask me in an irritated voice, "What are they up to now?"

By early 1961, the Tory party's fundamental weakness in Quebec was becoming more apparent. As the Union Nationale forces were declining, so the Lesage Liberals were riding high. My party was without a provincial base and I suggested to the party brass in Montreal that the time had come to form our own party within the province, but my proposals fell on deaf ears. Many of our Quebec members had strong attachments to the Union Nationale; others seemed uninterested. The same reason for doing nothing was given then as now: "The time is not ripe for such a move and such a party." I find this a lame response. Many of our federal MPs from Quebec who were elected in 1958 felt that theirs was a personal victory, that they had arrived in Ottawa largely as a result of their own efforts. This was not so; most of them had been swept in on the tide. But the lack of a provincial base for the party contributed to their defeat at the polls in 1962.

It seemed to me that two mutually exclusive currents were running through our party. One was Diefenbaker's loosely defined populism, which upset the old guard, who seemed to have a vested interest in keeping us in opposition. When we were on the opposition benches, this clique essentially ran the party. Dief's populism was suspect with the party establishment and while in power we were forever handing the opposition valuable ammunition. It was Progressive Conservative party supporters, mostly from central Canada, who started the personal attacks on Dief, as well as the cruel imitations. When his head shook on television, they said he was having a "jowel movement." They ridiculed him as they were later to ridicule Joe Clark, with equally disastrous results: it was Tories who labelled him "Joe Who?"

As 1962 got underway the Gallup poll indicated that 42% of voters would vote Liberal, compared to 36% for my party. The Liberal Opposition relentlessly attacked the Diefenbaker government's record on unemployment, as well the as the proposed increase in the old-age pension of a mere ten dollars a month. Diefenbaker had reneged on his 1958 promise to introduce a United States-type contributory pension.

The throne speech had all the markings of an election manifesto. At the end of January, the Liberal National Council adopted its economic platform. It was a conscious attempt to occupy the middle ground between the Tories and NDP and had been drafted by Maurice Lamontagne. The program called for full employment, acceptance that the government was directly responsible for monetary policy, an expansion of public services as a necessary investment in Canada's economic and social progress, establishment of a national economic council, a series of special measures to increase the markets for secondary manufacturing industries, more help for export industries, and credit for industry and consumers.

In mid-February, rumours of an impending election were rife. Diefenbaker wanted to call one soon, but Don Fleming, among others, favoured a later date. Then Diefenbaker started to play little games. He asked the Tory caucus and the press to be in the House late one Friday afternoon, but when they arrived he merely made an inconsequential announcement relating to a national power grid proposal. He left the House chuckling, leaving an unamused press gallery with pencils poised.

The 1962 Campaign

In mid-April Diefenbaker announced that June 18 was to be the day of reckoning. He said that originally he had chosen a later date, but Opposition obstruction had made him change his mind. The Liberals' manifesto soon hit the streets; it spelled out more than seventy election promises. On May 6, Diefenbaker officially launched his campaign before five thousand supporters in London, Ontario, where he pledged to review Canada's taxation system. As Diefenbaker began his speech, a television light popped. Loud applause and laughter greeted his ad lib: "This won't be the last explosion in this campaign!"

Then Fleming announced that the Government was devaluing the dollar; he had fixed the foreign exchange rate of the Canadian dollar at ninety-two and a half cents against the American dollar. It was the first time since 1950 that the government had undertaken to maintain the value of our dollar at a fixed rate. The move came less than a month after Fleming had explained in his budget speech why it was inappropriate for Canada to fix the exchange rate, as we had been urged to do for almost a year by the International Monetary Fund. Opposition spokesmen said that devaluation would immediately increase the cost of living because the price of imported goods would shoot up. Our large balance of payments deficit was there for all to see; Canadians were living well beyond their means.

Since October the treasury had poured $516 million of its American holdings into the exchange market to prevent the value of the Canadian dollar dropping below the ninety-five cent level. Large capital imports over a long period were, in part, responsible for the situation.

The floating rate of exchange policy was over. The timing of the decision and the rate adopted seemed to have been imposed on the government by external forces. The post-war honeymoon was coming to an end. As our trading partners became more self-reliant, they had less need for our goods and services.

The Opposition's broadsides began immediately. Walter Gordon said, "This is an awful time to do a thing like this. Mr. Fleming would not have done it unless the situation was out of control." He went on to say that the news would add to international nervousness about Canadian fiscal policies

The Liberal Opposition flooded the country with Diefendollars. These were replicas of the Canadian dollar only with a portion cut off at the end, dramatically demonstrating the effects of the devaluation. The press soon took up the slogan.

Over 80% of Canada's population lives within two hundred miles of the American border. The political implications of devaluation were immeasurable, especially in ridings along the border, and the rising political rhetoric deeply wounded the government, which went on to lose a record of nearly a hundred seats. I believe that Diefenbaker's gutsy performance on the hustings saved the government from a rout and allowed it to continue in a minority situation after the election. It is incredible to think Fleming decided to devalue in the middle of a campaign, without the matter being discussed by the full cabinet and caucus. Yet, this indicates how immune from the real world were the finance mandarins.

As the 1962 campaign came to an end, Diefenbaker drove from Ottawa to the West Island of Montreal for a luncheon meeting to support the candidacy of the sitting member, Marcel Bourbonnais. Afterwards, the prime minister invited me to join him and his wife on the drive to my riding, where he was to speak on my behalf at the Cowansville Town Hall. As usual with Dief, the conversation en route was animated. The prime minister ate one candy after another and when we arrived at our destination, the floor of the car was covered with discarded wrappers. He was pessimistic about the outcome of the election, so much so that he suggested that we would not even be able to form a minority government. His pessimism was well-founded. Diefenbaker told me that he had canvassed the cabinet before he saw the governor general, in order to determine whether or not any troublesome issues were in the wind. When he asked cabinet members about the advisability of calling an election, Diefenbaker claimed that nothing had ever been mentioned about the pegging of the dollar.

On the outskirts of Cowansville, we were met by a marching band that led us to the Town Hall. A young teenager on a ten-speed bicycle approached our car to get a good look at the prime minister. To do this, the young boy had thrown his bike out of gear, and had to peddle madly to keep his balance. The bicycle remained almost stationary as the frenzied peddling took place. Dief peered out of the car, watching the forward peddling that was creating no advance motion, and quipped, "He's going nowhere, just like our campaign."

On June 3, in Chelmsford, Ontario, three thousand screaming demonstrators nearly turned a political gathering for Dief and his wife into a riot. The demonstration was really against Roland Gillis, the local Tory candidate and president of the Local 598 of the International Union of Mines, Mill and Smelter Workers. Gillis wanted the local to join the United Steelworkers of America, but the workers in the Nickel Belt would have none of it. His unpopularity rubbed off on Dief.

A few days before, in Vancouver, seven thousand people had jammed into the Exhibition Forum. Fistfights broke out during Diefenbaker's speech, and placard-waving demonstrators shouted angrily about the Diefenbaker government's record. Howard Green, Minister of External

Affairs, tried to bring the meeting to order, but the hecklers shouted him down. National publicity from the meetings in Nickel Belt and Vancouver did a great deal of harm to our cause.

In my own riding, I could see that I had a tough fight on my hands.

At the end of May, Walter Gordon, one of the Liberal's leading spokesmen on economic affairs, proposed a six-point program. He said:

> 1) We cannot continue to go into debt to the tune of one billion dollars every year. We shall have to produce some of the things we have been importing.
>
> 2) Canadian industry must become more efficient. It may mean greater production in fewer plants if costs are to be kept in line.
>
> 3) Canadian industry should be offered tax incentives for increasing export sales.
>
> 4) Sooner or later the budget must be balanced.
>
> 5) One of the quickest ways of giving a stimulus to the Canadian economy in present circumstances will be to make funds available to the municipalities at moderate rates of interest.
>
> 6) There must be revisions in the tax system.

Early in the evening of election day it was apparent that the Conservatives were being badly beaten in Quebec and we were sustaining heavy losses nationally. As my early returns came in, I went ahead of Liberal candidate Marc Hudon by five hundred votes, and each subsequent phone call confirmed that I was maintaining this margin. When it became obvious that my lead would hold up, Hudon graciously phoned to concede defeat. Normand Ruel, the Créditiste candidate, had picked up nearly four thousand votes; a later analysis determined that his votes had eaten away at my former majority. The Liberal vote remained largely stable. Three

Quebec ministers—Hamilton, Flynn and Dorion—went down that night, and we were reduced to just fourteen seats in the province, compared with thirty-five for the Liberals and an astounding twenty-six for the Créditistes. Nationally, one hundred and fourteen Tories were returned, ninety-seven Liberals, plus thirty Social Credit and nineteen NDP members. While the West held relatively firm, we were slaughtered in Quebec and Ontario. The NDP had doubled its 1958 vote, gaining three seats in Metro Toronto, including David Lewis in York South. The first of two fatal blows had been struck at Diefenbaker and his government that was now reduced to minority status.

Chapter Two

The Diefenbaker Years 1963-1967

During the 1958 Parliament, Diefenbaker had reneged on his promise to appoint me a parliamentary secretary. At this time, an incident took place that had afforded me an insight into Diefenbaker's character and into one of the principal reasons for his downfall—his mishandling of people. He had not learned his lesson. In early August 1962 he wrote to me to say that he would like to make me a parliamentary secretary; would I write back listing the ministries in which I would prefer to serve? This I did, adding the following postscript: "If none of the above fits in with your plans, I would consider another ministry, with the exception of finance, for which I feel unsuited and which I do not want."

Soon afterwards, I received a summons to come to 24 Sussex Drive after breakfast. I met the prime minister in a small office just off the front hall. Papers were strewn everywhere, and Dief, hobbling on a broken ankle, was in a terrible mood. He started off by lecturing me in a hurt tone of voice "Why do you not want to be my parliamentary secretary?" I told him that being his own parliamentary secretary had been at the top of the list I had sent to him. The prime minister denied that he had got my letter and continued to harangue me. What could I say? At this point a maid entered the room, carrying a tray on which was piled a heap of documents. She handed the prime minister my letter. Dief grabbed the letter and read it quickly. "Well, well," he mumbled. Silence reigned for some time before he asked, "Would you like to be my parliamentary secretary?" I accepted willingly and Diefenbaker told me to report to him at the East Block in ten days.

I knew that the job would be a formidable one but I welcomed the challenge. Having observed the prime minister over the years, I had some strong misgivings, but for all his inexplicable manoeuvring, I still continued to prefer Dief to the elitist forces that were continually plotting against him.

I went back to Knowlton to rest before assuming my new duties. The pace over the past months had been hectic. A few days later, the prime minister's office rang. Diefenbaker was soon on the line, booming out, "I have good news for you. I want to make you a parliamentary secretary." I couldn't understand what was going on. Had he forgotten our meeting at Sussex Drive? He explained: "George Nowlan wants a bilingual parliamentary secretary at finance, especially to deal with Caouette and his funny-money theories. I want you to help George out." I reminded him of my letter in which I had said "anything but finance." This intervention triggered one of his infamous temper tantrums. He told me how ungrateful I was. "I'm having a press conference in a few minutes," the prime minister bellowed. "If you persist in your attitude, I guess you just won't be on the list of parliamentary secretaries." I backed off and accepted. For months afterwards in the government lobby behind the Commons chamber, Dief would remind me what good training ground the Department of Finance was for a young parliamentarian. In many ways, he was right. Working for Nowlan proved to be a fascinating and demanding experience.

At the end of August, the national executive and the party caucus met in Ottawa. There was a lot of internal criticism of party organization during the recent election. The same day, Diefenbaker announced that Kenneth Carter would head a royal commission to scrutinize the Canadian tax structure. This initiative had been promised by the Government for quite a while. It was clear after the party meeting that time was running out for us to complete our legislative agenda before the forthcoming session of Parliament.

George Nowlan was still being touted as a possible new leader. Things got so bad that Gordon Churchill asked me to keep a weather eye open and report any goings-on to him. Gordon considered me to be a Diefenbaker loyalist, but I had no intention of getting involved in anything furtive.

About this time, the Glassco Royal Commission published its first report on government organization. The commission pointed out the incredible waste of resources in government, ascribing it to the public services' slack and hidebound administrative procedures. As is the case today, projects whose raison d'être had disappeared were allowed to continue. At the end of November, Diefenbaker announced that the government would adopt most of the recommendations of the Glassco Report and named Senator Wallace McCutcheon to direct the overhaul of government administration.

Early in September 1962 Diefenbaker travelled to London for a Commonwealth conference. He and Nehru led the attack against Britain's entry into the Common Market; they and other nations declared that if Britain went in "under present proposals," it would be disastrous for most member countries. Macmillan was forced to call an emergency cabinet meeting to rethink his country's application. Back home, Pearson and Douglas sharply attacked Diefenbaker's criticism of Britain's proposal to join the European Community.

Two years earlier, Reginald Maudling's speech in Westminster conceded that if Britain went into Europe, its relationship with the Commonwealth would be drastically altered. Europe was marching towards political union, said Maudling, who was to become Chancellor of the Exchequer. "What," Diefenbaker asked in London "has happened in the intervening years to change the view of the British government?" If Britain joined the Common market, she would be unable to sign commercial treaties with Commonwealth partners, since these would be in the hands of the European Commission.

The British press accused the Canadian delegation of stonewalling. The opposition parties back in Ottawa contrived to exploit the situation by labelling Diefenbaker as unfriendly to "the mother country." The Suez debate had taught Pearson where the votes were; the sweet smell of power began to offset his loftier sensitivities.

African leaders warned that Britain's entry under the present proposals would enhance the western military alliance, and so offend their neutralist position. But it was obvious that Macmillan was determined to lead Britain into Europe. The Commonwealth leaders simply had to agree to disagree and hope that the passage of time would bring changes for the better. Not one of them budged an inch during the debate in London and the conference ended in a stalemate. I followed the proceedings closely with George Nowlan and, together with other cabinet members and the party faithful, we turned up to greet Dief on his return. This gathering of the clan at Ottawa's Uplands airport was calculated to boost our leader's sagging morale as he got ready to lead a minority Parliament.

Before the new session began, Lester B. Pearson started to flex his new-found political muscle, and he urged the collective opposition members to defeat the government as soon as possible. Bob Thompson cautioned his Social Credit followers that any party that precipitated an early election would incur the wrath of an unforgiving electorate.

After the nomination of Marcel Lambert as Speaker, the speech from the throne was read by Governor General Georges Vanier on September 27. The highlights were establishing an Atlantic development board to help promote economic development in the Atlantic provinces, balancing the budget, helping employees and workers meet the challenge of automation, and setting up a national medical research council.

In October 1962, the Cuban Missile Crisis made relations between Diefenbaker and the White House plummet further than ever. It could be argued that there was some merit in the basic principles of the prime minister's position, but the Liberals easily exploited the political opportunities inherent in deteriorating relations with our closest ally. Our minority situation was proving to be untenable.

The Cuban crisis revealed the rebelliousness of the Canadian military. Senior officials in the Department of National Defence went beyond their authority by ordering our forces on high alert without cabinet approval. By this time, Doug Harkness and Howard Green were barely talking; Harkness had little patience for Dief's fence-sitting at a time of crisis. Our ambassador in Washington, Charles Ritchie, subsequently informed me that he had been left completely in the dark about what was going on between Ottawa and the White House. Ritchie said the Canadian military were and are still quite capable of exceeding their authority under the same or other circumstances. George Ignatieff, our ambassador at the United Nations, knew no more than Ritchie. While all America's allies were speaking out clearly against the Soviets for putting missiles on Cuban soil, Diefenbaker had demanded an objective verification from neutral sources. Ignatieff had to sit in silence at the UN while Washington's other allies rushed in with their support.

After the release of documents under the Official Secrets Act, Robert Winters wrote in the Montreal *Gazette* (September 29, 1984):

> During the 1962 Cuban missile crisis, Canada's military leaders exceeded their authority by placing the armed forces on high alert—following the Pentagon's lead—despite the wishes of the federal cabinet headed by Prime Minister John Diefenbaker, who was suspicious of U.S. motives. It is one of the best-kept secrets of the last twenty years that at the height of the crisis Diefenbaker told a 25 October cabinet meeting that no action was to be taken to put Canadian forces on an alert footing without his approval. On 24 October, the cabinet had put off until its 25 October meeting the question of changing the alert status of Canadian forces—rejecting a recommendation by Defence Minister Douglas Harkness, who warned that Canada faced "the greatest danger" since the Second World War.

The military had clearly acted inappropriately. In his television address of October 22, Kennedy proclaimed a U.S. naval quarantine of Cuba. On October 9, Diefenbaker, asked in the Commons to comment on "a special report made to the State Department in Washington by the United States Maritime Administration on ... the part being played by eight Canadian-owned ships in trade between Communist countries and Cuba," replied:

Canada is not directly involved in this matter. We have been informed of the recent United States shipping regulations relative to trade with Cuba, but so far as I know there are no ships of Canadian registry that would be affected. Canada, as the House knows, does not permit the export to Cuba of arms or strategic materials. That is the basis of Canadian policy on this question, and it is not affected in any way by the activities of these ships ... which, as I stated earlier, under maritime law and general international law, are subject to the laws of the country under whose flag they operate. The eight ships in question are under British registry and, I again state, are not subject to Canadian laws or regulations.

Canadian–U.S. relations were reaching an all-time low. Kennedy thought Diefenbaker had let him down during a moment of need.

By mid-November it was apparent that the Liberals badly wanted an election. They had brought the business of the House to a halt. Pearson called for one vote of confidence after another.

On November 14, 1962 a provincial election was held in Quebec. Jean Lesage staked his political future on the nationalization of the electricity companies, while the main platform of Daniel Johnson's Union Nationale was lower taxes. During the campaign, Canada's first televised political debate took place as Lesage and Johnson squared off. The Lesage Liberals were swept back to power, gaining eleven seats over their 1960 total of fifty-two. The next Tory caucus was a pretty glum affair. Then on November 19, the Smallwood Liberals regained power in Newfoundland, taking thirty-three of the forty-two seats.

Obviously unhappy with his diminished federal role, Davie Fulton announced at the end of the month that he intended to run for leadership of the BC Progressive Conservative party.

Provincial elections ran into the month of December. Duff Roblin's majority in Manitoba was slightly reduced on December 14, just a few days before Premier Walter Shaw of Prince Edward Island led his

Conservative forces to victory for a second consecutive term.

Bilingualism at the Canadian National Railways became an issue in the fall. Fifty Quebec MPs tabled a resolution that called for more francophones to be appointed to executive positions at CNR. After appearing before a parliamentary committee, Donald Gordon, the CNR's president, was accused of bigotry when he intimated that there was a shortage of francophone talent from which to choose. Montreal students burned Gordon in effigy and marched in protest downtown. Gordon claimed that the Quebec education system was to blame and suggested that a royal commission should look into the whole matter of bilingualism.

In my talks with the prime minister, I soon learned that he did not support such a royal commission. When he was asked in the House if he would support a royal commission on bilingualism, Diefenbaker summarily brushed off the questioner with a quick "No." Opposition members used question period to highlight what they saw as Dief's anti-French bias.

On December 21, 1962 in Nassau, John F. Kennedy and Britain's Prime Minister Harold Macmillan announced that their countries would contribute some of their strategic nuclear powers to NATO and that Britain would hand over to the alliance a Polaris submarine force it was to obtain. A bilateral start had been made in creating a multilateral deterrent force within NATO that Washington had presented as the alternative to proliferation of national nuclear forces.

Diefenbaker flew to Nassau and lunched with Kennedy and Macmillan. Britain's difficulty in negotiating its entry into the Common Market was a topic for discussion at a meeting between Diefenbaker and Macmillan, but the British prime minister treated Dief with studied aloofness. The Cuban crisis had also created a further rift with Kennedy, and the opposition in Ottawa alleged that Diefenbaker was "a gate crasher," who had gone to Nassau uninvited.

As 1962 wound to an end, the Government was in deep trouble and so was I in my riding. Diefenbaker did not have a national theme for the imminent campaign. I had no local theme. My holiday visits to friends and relatives at the end of the year made it clear to me that I would have to work hard for re-election. I would also have to do quite a few things differently. I needed a theme and direction for my local campaign, and I needed to explain and defend Government policies.

The Final Curtain

"Never let your dreams turn into a nightmare," was a bit of advice given to me at an early age. In the first weeks of 1963, I witnessed an embittered prime minister fighting for his survival. Slowly but surely *his* dream was turning into a nightmare. As prime minister of a majority government from 1958 to 1962, he bore the major responsibility for our decline into a minority situation. Yet it is my firm conviction that his tough campaigning in 1962 saved our party. While the electorate had their misgivings about Diefenbaker, they did not wish fully to entrust majority power to Pearson.

In the first days of January 1963, I kept hoping that we could postpone the election until we had a more positive record to put before the electorate. The roof fell in after a series of confidence votes, an unbelievable fiasco on nuclear policy, a number of cabinet resignations, and finally the prime minister's unwillingness to iron out differences with Réal Caouette, when his Créditistes voted against the Diefenbaker government on a crucial vote of confidence. January and early February was a time of high political drama. Ottawa did not seem to be in the real world, and Parliament Hill was cocooned in an aura of make-believe.

At the beginning of January, in a luncheon address to the York Scarborough Liberal Association, Pearson re-emphasized his party's about-face on the question of nuclear warheads for Canadian forces. He then implied that, although as prime minister he would accept the warheads, he would attempt to negotiate Canada out of its commitment to retain them. The Government itself was still divided on the issue.

On January 25, Diefenbaker informed the Commons that Canada's role in the NATO alliance would be clarified at a NATO ministerial meeting in Ottawa in May. Meanwhile, he revealed that his government had been negotiating with Washington for the past two or three months for a scheme that would make nuclear warheads available for the armed forces in case they were needed. In the debate on defence and foreign policy, Diefenbaker declared: "More and more the nuclear deterrent is becoming of such nature that more nuclear arms will add nothing materially to out defenses. Greater and greater emphasis must be placed on conventional arms and conventional forces."

In contrast, Pearson said that it was humiliating and dishonorable for Canada to make pledges and accept nuclear commitments, and refuse to discharge them. On January 28, Doug Harkness took it upon himself to issue a statement clarifying Diefenbaker's speech, but this merely provoked further confusion, leading Paul Martin to call for the defence minister's resignation. The fat was in the fire. On January 30, the American State department said that the Canadian government had not yet proposed any arrangement for arming Canadian forces with nuclear weapons that would contribute effectively to the defence of North America.

At this time, I was comparatively detached from the main drama, busily helping George Nowlan to prepare his budget. Charles Ritchie was recalled from Washington to review the situation. In the House, Pearson sprang to the attack, waving the American statement at Diefenbaker and demanding an explanation. Diefenbaker replied testily that his speech did not need clarification and, in a dig at Kennedy, added that the Canadian government was not participating in "the new frontier." I was not prepared for the statement Harkness read to the House on February 14:

> Yesterday I sent to the Prime Minister my resignation as minister of National Defence.
>
> I believe it is the duty of a minister of National Defence to ensure the security of Canada to the greatest extent that he believes to be possible, on the basis of the information and advice he receives. I have always believed, in the pursuit of this duty as minister, that we should have nuclear weapons.

In all the defence negotiations concerning nuclear weapons in which I have had a part, the sovereignty of Canada has been protected fully. We have never lost sight of the dignity or independence of this country. ... Subsequently it became apparent to me that the Prime Minister's views on nuclear arms and my own are irreconcilable. On reflection, I believe now I made a mistake in agreeing to what would amount to be a four-month delay in obtaining nuclear warheads. I differ from the Prime Minister in this way—that I believe we should have obtained nuclear warheads for our weapons carriers as soon as the latter were ready. I thought throughout that by remaining in the cabinet I could better achieve this purpose than by taking the easier course of resigning.

I resigned on a matter of principle. The point was finally reached when I considered that my honour and integrity required that I take this step....

I should like to make it clear that I absolutely reject the position on nuclear weapons set forth by the Liberal leader—that anomalous position in that Canada should never evade her responsibility by accepting nuclear weapons now, and then immediately negotiating out of them.

Never in the history of Canadian-American relations had there been such an open disagreement between Ottawa and Washington. It constituted an open intervention into Canada's affairs by an otherwise friendly neighbour. Early in February, *Newsweek* magazine published a vicious attack on Diefenbaker, coupled with a photograph of him taken through a light globe while he was speaking. The effect distorted the prime minister's head, making him look like an imbecile. The intemperate language of the article aroused furious editorial reaction in Canada.

Rumours continued to sweep Parliament Hill. While Social Credit Leader Bob Thompson said that he wanted to see a Liberal vote of confidence motion before deciding whether or not to support it, some cabinet members already had serious doubts about Diefenbaker's leadership, and they met privately on the first Sunday in February. The group included Wallace McCutcheon, George Nowlan, Davie Fulton, Ernest Halpenny, and Léon Balcer. Afterwards, they saw Diefenbaker at 24 Sussex and told him they wanted to solve the defence-policy question before embarking on an election.

The nuclear issue was not the only item of interest during this time. André Laurendeau, editor of *Le Devoir*, signed an editorial on January 19 calling for what amounted to a commission on bilingualism and biculturalism, largely supporting Pearsons's stand on the matter. In the House, Lionel Chevrier, a former Liberal transport minister and father of the St. Lawrence Seaway, asked the prime minister if he would support such a proposition. Diefenbaker replied that the government favored an alternative route, such as a national conference. Chevrier pounced on Diefenbaker's reply and painted him as an unsympathetic anti-Quebecer. This was not Chevrier at his best.

By early February 1963, it seemed as if we would soon be plunged into yet another election. Two non-confidence motions, one sponsored by the Liberals and the other by the Socreds, were introduced into the House on February 4. On the same day, David Lewis offered some short-term respite for the government, calling the Liberals "power mad."

The battle lines were drawn. In his Commons' speech on the motion of confidence, Pearson inexplicably pleaded with Diefenbaker not to make a political football out of the nuclear issue. "No government," he said, "has any right to go on sitting, having failed so lamentably and miserably to govern." The Liberal motion of confidence read:

> This government, because of lack of leadership, the breakdown of unity in the cabinet and confusion and indecision in dealing with national and international problems, does not have the confidence of the Canadian people.

Originally, Bob Thompson promised that he would support the minority government by voting against the Liberal motion. He then began to skate, saying he was stalling in order to establish a firm caucus position. The Socred caucus had set out four conditions on which it would support the Government: a clear-cut statement of defence policy; introduction of the 1963-64 spending estimates within two weeks; the tabling of a new budget within four weeks, with an eight-day debate to follow; and a "positive program of follow-up action respecting many things for which Parliament had already given authority."

Thompson acknowledged that an election would be a disaster, but put his party's motion of confidence before the House:

> This government has failed up to this time to give a clear statement of policy respecting Canada's national defence, and has failed to organize the business of the House so that the 1963-64 estimates and budget could be introduced and does not have the confidence of the Canadian people.

On February 5, Diefenbaker made a fighting speech in the House. He said that he had entertained the thought of an election, but felt that the people of Canada "wanted us to get our legislation through."

There are many conflicting views of what happened during the supper hour following that afternoon sitting. Here is my version. There was still hope for the government. Réal Caouette wanted to confer privately with Diefenbaker; he wished to save face and tell his troops that the prime minister had listened constructively to his views and proposals. There was only one problem: Diefenbaker would not receive Caouette and none of his colleagues could persuade him to do so. As the hour approached for the House to resume sitting that evening, George Nowlan asked Caouette whether a conversation with him would suffice. "You're a good cardinal," replied Caouette, "but I must see the pope." Yet a stubborn prime minister refused Caouette an audience. It was vintage Diefenbaker in one of his increasingly frequent bouts of pure bloody-mindedness. That evening the vote was taken and the government collapsed. On both the Socred sub-amendment and the Liberal amendment, the combined opposition totalled 142 votes. Two New Democrats, Bert Herridge and Colin Cameron, voted with the 109 Conservatives. There was pandemonium as Diefenbaker moved the adjournment. The clock had been turned back thirty-seven years. At 2 a.m. on July 22, 1926, the Meighen government was defeated by one vote, only because a Progressive member had inadvertently broken his pair. (Pairing constitutes an informal tradition where, for example, government members will only absent themselves from a House vote if they are paired with an opposition member who will also refrain from voting.)

I was emotionally exhausted. We had gone down, unnecessarily, because a proud prime minister would not confer with a leading member of the opposition. The day after the vote, Diefenbaker announced that the Governor General had dissolved the eight-month old Parliament.

George Nowlan continued to be touted as a replacement for Diefenbaker, but after the next caucus, Nowlan said to reporters: "The Party was never more excellent. I have always respected caucus secrecy. Suffice it to say that the Wednesday caucus was the most emotional one I ever attended. Grown men shed tears as they pledged loyalty to their leader." Outside, Diefenbaker asked George Hees to tell reporters about it all. "I am the caucus chairman and I can say that it was a wonderful caucus," exclaimed Hees. "We're on the road and we're going to knock the hell out of the Grits and we're going to win the election."

However, it was an open secret there had been a cabinet revolt over what many felt was Diefenbaker's indecision on the nuclear issue and on economic issues, especially those to do with the dollar crisis. At a time when tough decisions were needed, the dissidents felt that Dief had continued to emulate the government style of "Old Tomorrow," Sir John A. Macdonald, and Mackenzie King.

Gordon Churchill, Alvin Hamilton, and Howard Green led the cabinet loyalists. On the night of the vote, Hamilton gathered a number of loyal members in the government lobby. In the House, Diefenbaker was talking with Green and Waldo Montieth. Hamilton urged his leader to go out to the lobby, where he was greeted by an overwhelming show of support. I was there and ready to fight. In politics you make choices. Diefenbaker's warts were there for all to see, but I preferred him to the elitist forces that had never become reconciled to his leadership in the first place.

There is nothing like an election to unite the troops. You can think what you like about your leader, but if it becomes known by your constituents that you are disloyal, I know no better formula for political extinction. That is not to condone blind subservience to the leader, nor to declare that you should not resign over what you feel is a matter of deep personal conviction. It does mean, however, that once you have had your say in caucus, you then back your leader. The system demands it and the electorate seeks the same stability. Unfortunately, members of my party have only recently understood this basic principle. In Canada we vote for the leader and the candidate on the same ballot. By damning your leader, you have simultaneously confirmed an elector's possible dislike of him and demonstrated personal disloyalty. Come election day, this same constituent will not put her or his cross by your name.

On the weekend following the government's defeat, George Hees and Pierre Sévigny handed in their resignations. A week later Donald Fleming announced he was quitting after twenty-five years of public life. Diefenbaker moved to repair the damage, naming Gordon Churchill as defence minister and Speaker Marcel Lambert as minister of veterans affairs. Much to the surprise of most observers, Senator Wallace McCutcheon took over from Hees as minister of trade and commerce. Later on in the campaign, the prime minister made Martial Asselin, defeated in the June election, minister of forestry. In March, Frank McGee was promoted to minister without portfolio as was my good friend Théogène Ricard. By then, Ernest Halpenny had announced his impending retirement for health reasons.

So we were off and running. If they were elected, the Liberals promised sixty days of decision, based on President Kennedy's famous election promise. With Judy LaMarsh at the helm, the Grits announced the establishment of a "truth squad," to follow Dief on the hustings, but, as we shall see later, the whole thing was a storm in a teacup.

I returned immediately to my riding. My first greeting in Farnham offered little encouragement. "Why don't you quit like Sévigny?" a Liberal asked me before turning his back and moving off. I determined to organize and work hard, visiting thousands of homes, factories, stores, and public places. If I was tired, I didn't know it.

As the campaign got underway, Diefenbaker announced the Conservative party platform: "The Progressive Conservative party is now placing before the Canadian people a program of national purpose." The platform listed the following aims:

1) Achieve a sense of national unity and purpose.

2) Continue economic growth.

3) Act on urban renewal.

4) Develop a national power grid.

5) Expand national agriculture program.

6) Increase vocational training.

7) Extend social security.

8) Strive for world peace and disarmament.

Earlier, the Liberals had put forward the broad lines of its platform:

1) Create a new federal department of industry.

2) Create a municipal development and loan fund.

3) Lower interest rates.

4) Establish of a national health insurance plan and a contributory old-age pension plan.

5) Continue family allowances while children remain in high school.

6) Accept current defence commitments, followed by a review of Canadian policy.

7) Preserve the family farm.

8) Establish a federal labour code, providing a minimum hourly wage of $1.25, a maximum work week of forty hours, a minimum paid vacation of two weeks, seven

statutory holidays with pay; recognition of the right to strike, collective bargaining for civil servants, and 9) establishment of a national economic council.

I began to sense that my campaign was going well. Like Dief, I was an underdog. If Diefenbaker was an indecisive prime minister, he was nevertheless a great campaigner. Without him, the Grits would have had a working majority in 1962. Although he was unpopular in the major cities of Quebec, many rural people admired his toughness and willingness to hang in. Even though he spoke laughable French, a host of rural Quebecers gave him grudging admiration.

In February 1963, in Washington, Charles Ritchie conferred with Dean Rusk on North American defence matters. He was understood to be reopening discussions on Ottawa's proposal to store nuclear warheads for the Bomarcs on the American side of the border. There was no indication that Washington would look upon this arrangement any more favourably than it had done when it had first been first broached several months before.

At the end of the month, Diefenbaker flew to London to receive The Freedom of the City. The Commonwealth was the theme of his acceptance speech at the Guildhall before a thousand distinguished guests, including Prime Minister Harold Macmillan. Diefenbaker noted that the base of the Commonwealth had been so broadened since the last war "that no full and democratic nation desiring to join us should or I think would be denied admission."

Diefenbaker read the lessons at the morning service at the City Temple before spending twenty minutes with Sir Winston Churchill at his home in Hyde Park Gate. On Saturday evening he had what was described as a working dinner with Macmillan and members of his cabinet, discussing trade and defence matters. The London interlude was soon over and the beleaguered leader returned to Canada to face the electorate.

Pearson started his campaign in Montreal on the last Saturday of

February, emphasizing his nuclear position and the need for Quebecers to play a broader role in Confederation. The nuclear issue was a tough one for him in Quebec; the Créditistes, for one, were against nuclear warheads on Canadian soil.

In the middle of March 1963, the Liberal truth squad came to a hasty end. The first confrontation between Diefenbaker and the squad took place in Moncton, and the prime minister enjoyed it immensely. The idea for the squad had been cooked up at Liberal headquarters without Pearson's approval, and he soon axed it. The other political parties reacted angrily to the idea of bringing a truth squad into the campaign. T. C. Douglas call it a "thoroughly un-Canadian and thoroughly reprehensible, Madison Avenue gimmick." Socred leader Robert Thompson said that he did not like this kind of politics because it destroyed the people's confidence in the political system.

Diefenbaker's meeting in Halifax seemed to be the last straw for the squad. They demanded police protection as the crowd chanted "Throw out Judy." Keith Davey saw his juvenile scheme turn sour. The same fate awaited Davey's scurrilous colouring books with their ill-fated humourous attacks on Diefenbaker and his government.

In Quebec, only Caouette seemed to be drawing the crowds. Gatherings at Pearson's and Diefenbaker's meetings dwindled as the campaign progressed. On the other hand, compared to 1962, the prime minister's campaign tour was excellent and things were going smoothly. Diefenbaker grabbed the theme of the Liberal obstruction at the outset and went on the attack.

Perhaps one of the most colourful aspects of the campaign in Quebec was the continued confrontation between the Liberal's Yvon Dupuis and the Caouette Créditistes. The meetings Dupuis addressed were usually stormy and attended by scores of Socred hecklers. Jean Lesage decided to hit out against the Créditistes.

Thompson and Caouette kicked off their respective campaigns with a large Montreal rally, while Tommy Douglas started out in Toronto calling for a national referendum on the nuclear issue. At the end of the campaign, the NDP had what was described as the largest rally ever in the history of Canada. Nearly sixteen thousand people crowded into Toronto's Maple Leaf Gardens. Douglas's speech was uneventful, but he got a great ovation when he outlined his party's policy on medicare.

In the last weeks of the campaign, the American defence secretary, Robert S. McNamara, testifying before a congressional committee, said the Bomarc bases could be expected to draw attacks from enemy missiles and thus divert them from more important targets. A great deal of confusion ensued over his views about their strategic usefulness, pushing our party leaders into a frenzied debate on the issue.

My big moment of the campaign came in the last week. The party organized a huge rally for the prime minister at Ste-Thérèse High School in Cowansville, complete with an old-fashioned supper of tourtière, pork and beans, hot rolls, coffee, and maple sugar pie. Twelve hundred people sat down for dinner.

Diefenbaker often used a train during the campaign and he and Olive arrived by rail in a snowstorm on April 2. My wife and I rode with them from the station to the hall. We were held up for a few moments as the mayor's car got stuck in the snow in front of us. It was a great meeting. The meal and decorations were excellent. Dief delivered a "stemwinding" speech which brought the audience to its feet more than once. There was only one disconcerting element. A hostile national press were sitting behind tables in the front row. They did everything but heckle Diefenbaker, grimacing and groaning out loud after he had delivered some of his telling sallies.

Once back at the station, I went on board the train to say goodbye to my leader. He had already retired for the evening, but Olive asked if I would go into the bedroom to say goodbye to him and give him a little boost. When I got to the door, he had already gone to bed. He looked exhausted, but had a broad smile on his face. Stretching out his arm to give me a good handshake, he congratulated me on my speech and asked me to convey his thanks to the party workers for organizing such a splendid event. "How did we do, Heward?" he asked. My broad smile gave him the answer and he reached up and touched my shoulder. I think he was almost asleep as I reached the door and turned around to give him a final wave. It was six days before the election and it would be the last time I would see him as prime minister. However, his speech had given the troops a great lift.

Election day was at hand, and, as usual after voting, I toured nearly all the polls to thank our workers. My top workers were Gaëtan Mireault and Louis Cournoyer. My strategy had paid off. When the results were in, I had tripled my 1962 majority, and had cut the Créditiste vote almost in half. But that was the only cause for celebration. We had elected only eight members in the province and the results elsewhere were disastrous. The only consolation was that, because of Diefenbaker's hard-hitting campaign, it looked as if Pearson would be held to a minority position. We won no seats in Metro Toronto. A solid block of Prairie support for Diefenbaker stopped Pearson from winning a majority, something that would elude him to the end of his stewardship. Canada had elected its third minority government in less than six years. The Liberals won 126 seats, to 94 for the Progressive Conservatives, 24 for the Social Credit, and 17 for the NDP. The Grits had taken seats from Caouette in Quebec. Speaking to the country on television from Prince Albert, Diefenbaker said, "I gave the best that was in me. I followed the course that was right."

The next day, Pearson said he was ready to speak as prime minister. I was to sit to the left of Mr. Speaker. With the exception of a nine-month interlude between 1979 and 1980, my party would sit in Opposition for the better part of another twenty-one years. For Diefenbaker and his government, this was really The End.

The 1963 Minority Liberal Government

As the 1963 government got under way, I was not surprised by the way senior bureaucrats openly welcomed Pearson and his team back to power. They made no pretence at hiding their joy as the Diefenbaker team went down.

What country in the free world would have tolerated what I witnessed from the Opposition benches? If only one ex-senior civil servant had adorned the Pearson minority government, that could have been understood—but across from me in the Government front benches sat not only Pearson, the ex-Under Secretary of Foreign Affairs, but also Bud Drury, the ex-deputy minister of national defence; Jack Pickersgill, ex-clerk of the Privy Council; and Mitchell Sharp, ex-deputy minister of Trade and Commerce. There were others.

The Liberal Government immediately addressed Medicare—giving universal health care coverage to all Canadians. Then there were the flag debate and the vote to end capital punishment. The red maple leaf flag was unfurled on Parliament Hill on February 15, 1965. These debates seriously divided the Tory caucus. Verbal exchanges behind the curtains of the Commons and in the Opposition lobby were incredibly harsh. The party's public image suffered.

My party in opposition created a set of circumstances which were ironic in the extreme. Pearson had a relatively strong set of Quebec ministers, notably Guy Favreau and Gilles Lamontagne. I don't believe for a minute there was an anti-Quebec bias in the Opposition attack on Quebec ministers. Led by Eric Nielsen on the Opposition benches, the credibility of the Liberal ministers from Quebec was effectively destroyed. Yvon Dupuis, the firebrand deputy from St-Jean, was implicated in a racetrack scandal. It was against the background of these events that Pearson and his advisers conscripted the three so-called wise men from Quebec: Marchand, Trudeau, and Pelletier, paving the way for Trudeau's eventual rise to the top. Pearson felt strongly that his eventual successor should be a Quebecer. Pearson was not all that keen on Trudeau, because of the latter's attack on him in the publication *Cité Libre*, although deep down I believe Pearson understood and respected Trudeau's opposition to the Bomarc missile. I leave it to you, the reader, to divine whether or not the eventual coronation of Trudeau would have taken place without the systematic destruction by the Opposition of Quebec ministers before the election of 1965.

The End of the Chief
The 1966 challenge to John Diefenbaker's leadership, orchestrated by the late Dalton Camp, president of the Progressive Conservative Party,

left the party divided between Diefenbakers's supporters and his enemies. Diefenbaker's critics generally espoused a more radical conservative philosophy than that practised by the leader. Furthermore, the mounting influence of western agrarianism in the formation of party policy was making Dief's opponents uneasy as they foresaw that it would lead to abandonment of the party by the central Canadian establishment. These two factors, coupled with some personal animosity directed at The Chief and his leadership style, fueled the rebels' efforts to depose him.

After several years of deeply divisive internal conflict, the 1966 annual meeting of the party directed the national executive to call a leadership convention before the end of 1967. The vote for a leadership convention was, in effect, a vote of non-confidence against Diefenbaker. There were nine contenders for the PC leadership in 1967. Besides Diefenbaker and Robert Stanfield, the field included former Manitoba premier Duff Roblin and six members of the federal cabinet—Davie Fulton, George Hees, Alvin Hamilton, Wallace McCutcheon, Donald Fleming, and Michael Starr. Starr and Hamilton had waited until late in the campaign before announcing their intention to run for the leadership. Both had waited until it appeared that Diefenbaker, whom they had supported against the challenge of the dissidents, would not join the race. Both felt certain they could count on Diefenbaker's support, but they had the rug pulled out from under them when Diefenbaker announced his intention to run for the leadership. The Chief would not go down easily.

Despite Diefenbakers's presence in the field, the race was really between Duff Roblin and Robert Stanfield. However, Roblin entered the race much later than he should have, out of his consideration for Diefenbaker. To have announced his intention to run early might have been construed as a slap in the face of the leader.

I personally supported Roblin and had conferred with him on numerous occasions before his official announcement. There were a number of reasons for my choice. The first was his ability to be understood in French. Unlike Stanfield, Roblin was well-liked in Quebec, and especially by Premier Daniel Johnson. Given that any future PC government would require significant support from Quebec, I felt that

Roblin's Quebec popularity was critical to the future success of the party. Coupling this with his record in Manitoba and his popularity among francophone Manitobans, I was sure Roblin was a winner. Although I did have some reservations about supporting a provincial premier rather than one of my caucus colleagues, the factionalism that was evident in our parliamentary ranks convinced me that the next leader of the party would have to come from outside the Commons.

As for Robert Stanfield, his decision to run for the leadership was a surprise to many people. When asked about his intentions shortly after Diefenbaker's electoral defeat, Stanfield answered that he would rather "take up ski jumping" than run for the leadership of the federal Tories, but ultimately he did join the race. His change of heart can be partially attributed to support he was promised by the dissident faction of the party. Dalton Camp was one of the prominent figures on the Stanfield team, personally contacting people at every level of the party for pledges of support. Flora MacDonald and Gordon Fairweather encouraged me, and others of their colleagues, to back Stanfield. I remained uncommitted, not convinced that Stanfield had the capacity to lead the party to national victory.

In April 1967, I traveled to Winnipeg to address a constituency meeting in St. Boniface. On the Saturday morning before the meeting, I met with Roblin, encouraging him to announce his intention to run as soon as possible. He told me to wait until mid-June; if he was willing to enter his name, he would let me know by then. Mid-June passed, and there was no word from Duff. I assumed that he had decided not to run.

In late August, the party held a policy conference at Montmorency, just outside Quebec City. Just after the conference got under way, Roblin announced his candidacy. I pledged my support for him immediately, but I knew that we were probably too late to mount a winning campaign. A few days later, on a highly publicized swing through Quebec, Roblin met only a handful of delegates. Even at that late date, most the Quebec delegates had not been named.

The delegate-selection meetings were being organized by the time that Roblin and Diefenbaker joined the race. Many of these meetings were being held without an adequate period of time for the candidates to raise their public profiles or to establish their stands on the issues. Delegates were being chosen who were uncommitted or had pledged to support a candidate they had not had a chance to meet and question. As in all previous leadership campaigns since the 1920s, delegate selection seemed like a mechanized process, unaffected by events that were taking place on the campaign trail.

Who were these delegates who were being selected to represent the party membership in the choice of party leader? They certainly did not represent the composition of the Progressive Conservative party. Over 40 % of the delegates had university degrees and a full 44 % had a family income of $15,000, which, in 1967 put them in a high-income bracket. Few delegates were union members or blue-collar workers.

Also unrepresentative of the party membership were all the ex officio delegates. These were people who had served the party either as MPs or as MPPs had presided over the youth wing or other party organizations, or worked at party headquarters of the delegates at the Toronto leadership convention. Ex officio delegates, representatives of what could only be termed the party elite, made up 46% of the total.

The delegations from many ridings also included blow-in delegates. Although it is impossible to accurately measure their numbers, they made up a sizeable portion of the delegates from Quebec. Blow-in delegates were acclaimed, rather than elected, at the riding level or nominated by the riding executive to fill delegate spots left vacant. In addition, the remaining vacancies were filled at the convention itself by convention organizers with delegates from other parts of the country. Thus it was that an alternate delegate from Northern Ontario might fill a vacancy in a delegation from east-end Montreal.

The 1967 Tory leadership race was the first in party history to be heavily bankrolled. No expense was spared by the front-runners in their cross-Canada campaign. The party executive was unprepared for this new American style of leadership campaign, and therefore had no rules in place to control the spending or ensure that all the contributions made to the candidates were fully reported.

Stanfield and Roblin battled through five ballots before Stanfield received the requisite number of votes to be declared the winner. The deciding factor in Stanfield's victory was the support he enjoyed among ex officio delegates and in the group led by Dalton Camp. While Roblin was the most popular candidate with the majority of Tory voters, especially in Quebec where Reine Gagné, Premier Johnson's widow, and Luce Pellant, Paul Sauvé's widow, endorsed him, the party brass was driving the Stanfield machine. The group had talked Stanfield into taking up the challenge of a leadership race, and they prepared the groundwork, raised the funds, and ensured the support before the lanky Nova Scotian announced that he would join the race. While the national press that gathered at the convention largely ignored the ex officio factor in Stanfield's victory, it was apparent to those on the floor that Roblin's defeat came at the hands of this segment of the delegates. Without calling into question Stanfield's abilities or his fine record as a legislator and premier, we can regret the fact that an unelected contingent, which made up nearly half of the assembled delegates, would undermine the working of democracy in the party's leadership-selection process.

After Stanfield was named leader, although Diefenbaker no longer was leader of the Opposition, he nevertheless had a front row seat in the Commons. Invariably, he would ask lengthy questions which by any normal standard were patently out of order. Because he was our ex-prime minister, the speaker let him get away with it. His questions were usually directed at Pierre Trudeau. I always felt that Trudeau was being somewhat patronizing towards Diefenbaker but I was mistaken. During subsequent meetings with Pierre, he told me he liked Diefenbaker and respected him. He said that when he worked for the Privy Council back in the mid-fifties, he often came to the House of Commons and sat in the visitors gallery where he watched the Dief in full flight. Trudeau told me he liked him because he felt Dief was on the side of those who needed help.

CHAPTER THREE

The Stanfield Years 1967-1976
(Three Strikes and Out)

"Two Nations" —Strike 1

In August 1967, just before the party's convention in Toronto that designated Bob Stanfield as its leader, I attended our policy conference in Montmorency, Quebec. It was there that I first heard of the policy initiative "Two Nations." I never knew what it meant and still don't. Nevertheless, it had a sort of pseudo-intellectual appeal to many influential people in the party—including Stanfield. For some reason, they felt "Two Nations" would appeal to the Quebec electorate—that is, if they could figure out what it meant.

Peter Lougheed, the new leader of the Tories in Alberta, was at the conference. I had met him in Edmonton the winter before, and was full of admiration for his centrist stand on most issues. It is my view even today in 2002 that Peter could be a huge and central force in rebuilding our party fortunes in the West. At the conference, he was enraged and went into orbit at the thought of "Two Nations" which he claimed would be anathema to most westerners. At the same meeting, Dick Bell, our member from Ottawa-Carleton, and Marcel Faribeault, one of the principal instigators of the new policy, got into an ugly shouting match over the issue. I sensed that we were sowing yet another seed of political disaster. The problem, as I well knew, is that nation meant one thing in English and another in French. In English, "nation" has a well-defined political connotation, while in French, the context for "nation" is largely social. Not to worry. The party elite plunged ahead. Diefenbaker was the first, with his well-publicized views on "one Canada" and his attack what he conceived to be a dangerous and divisive policy. "Two Nations" did not go over well with Canadian voters and divided the party.

After the leadership convention, the House met in the fall. The steam was running out of Pearson's minority government and things looked reasonable for us. During the winter months, it became apparent to me that Diefenbaker was undermining our new leader—that his western loyalists had not accepted Stanfield. Also, it seemed to me that Stanfield was over his head when it came to dealing with party organization in Quebec.

After Lester Pearson resigned, a Liberal convention named Pierre Trudeau as party leader. This meant he became prime minister. He dissolved the House on April 23, 1968 and called an election for June 25. Throughout this book, I often refer to Pierre Trudeau. My friendship with him dates back long before either of us entered public life. We did not agree on all things political. While I've always been very circumspect in talking or writing about my many meetings with Pierre and our great friendship, there is one thing I feel the public and my readers should know about him that is not generally recognized. Pierre was a strong Roman Catholic. He often attended mass at the Franciscan Church on René-Lévesque Boulevard near Atwater Avenue in Montreal. At his son Michel's memorial mass, Pierre read from the Old Testament. Resurrection was the central theme of the reading.

I had a lunch engagement with Pierre a few days after Michel was killed and phoned Anne Paris, his secretary, to cancel the luncheon after I heard the news. She told me that Pierre still wanted to get together. I met him at his law office. He was looking very sad. On the way to lunch, I asked him, "What event in history would you like to have witnessed?"

"My God, Heward," he replied, "that's the kind of question you would ask. What about you?"

I said my choice was the Last Supper.

After much reflection he turned to me and said, "My choice would be the Resurrection."

"But Pierre," I replied, "there was no one there."

He said, "I know that, but I would still like to have been there."

I think this little anecdote tells a lot about my friend Pierre. I miss him very much.

During the early fifties when I was a law student at McGill, I would see Pierre at formal balls. This invariably involved men in white-tie evening suits and tails and women in long dresses and corsages. Pierre was ten years older than most of us at that time but he enjoyed partying. For him, going to mass every Sunday was a must, but after arriving home at around 4 a.m. he didn't like to get up for mass after only a few hours sleep. At one point, he found out that the Franciscan monks celebrated mass at 4:30 Sunday mornings. Pierre often attended the balls with his sister, Suzette, and they once arrived at the Franciscan church for the 4:30 mass still dressed in their evening clothes. While the monks were a little surprised, they welcomed Pierre and his sister. This solved the problem of going to bed late on a Saturday night and getting up Sunday for morning mass.

We were badly organized in Quebec and Stanfield named Marcel Faribeault as his Quebec lieutenant—a ludicrous move that caused much resentment in our Quebec caucus. Faribeault, a reserved patrician, was unelectable. Party organizers took him to his new-found riding, Gamelin in the east end of Montreal. When he was told he would have to shake hands with the voters, he was horrified and quit the hustings for good. Leaders with no real understanding of the Quebec scene felt obliged, in the past, to name lieutenants to conduct party and government affairs in Quebec. The validity of the lieutenancy principle in Quebec had long since passed. After the sudden death of Ernest Lapointe in World War II, Mackenzie King hastened to enlist Louis St-Laurent from Quebec City. When the latter became prime minister, the lieutenancy rule died. Stanfield chose to ignore this fact.

Trudeaumania had hit the land. I was out of step with the times and never knew what Trudeaumania had to do with issues and the substance of governing. The newly-minted prime minister was seen kissing teenagers and doing flips off diving boards, while the press featured a picture of Stanfield fumbling a football. The caption read, "Stanfield fumbles again." This was grossly unfair because Bob, a good athlete, had caught a number of passes, but the cameras only clicked when he finally fumbled. The wind was in Trudeau's sails.

The Sunday night before the elections Trudeau's luck still held. With Mayor Jean Drapeau of Montreal and Quebec premier Daniel Johnson, Trudeau was in the St-Jean Baptiste parade when radical separatists started to throw missiles at them. Drapeau and Johnson beat a hasty retreat, while Trudeau defiantly stood his ground. The publicity for Trudeau on election day, standing up to the separatists and staring them down, spoke for itself.

Election Day—June 25, 1968—brought bad news for my party. The result: a majority government for Trudeau and the Liberals. "Two Nations" played into Trudeau's hand and, in my view, significantly affected the results at the polls. Stanfield had nailed his campaign to the "Two Nations" plank. He went down to defeat and swung at the ball for Strike 1.

"Wagner, c'est vrai"—Strike 2

In September of 1968 Stanfield had named me Opposition spokesman for the Hellyer Task Force on Housing. Paul Hellyer was the minister in charge of housing initiatives. A number of distinguished Canadians participated in the task force hearings that were held from coast to coast. I learned a lot about the intransigence of the Canadian civil service.

Thanks to the courtesy of Lloyd Axworthy, Hellyer's executive assistant, space was made for me on the government plane carrying the task force panel. Many first class and imaginative suggestions to fine-tune and improve housing policy were put forward. Travelling with us were officials from the Canada Mortgage and Housing Corporation. I could not help but overhear their negative observations about the hearings. Little did I realize at the time the influence they would have in the ultimate disposition of hearing recommendations. At each stop the media interviewed me. I did my best to reply to questions without being overly partisan. When the task force completed its tour of Canada, I arranged a fifteen-minute television spot showing Stanfield visiting housing units and offering positive commentary on housing matters. The spot was aired on the networks and was a great success.

The point of this story relates to what happened next. After Hellyer's recommendations were presented to cabinet they were turned down. The prime mover in killing the recommendations in cabinet was Mitchell Sharp. Officials from CMHC and other bureaucrats involved in housing policy caught Sharp's attention. Sharp, the former senior civil servant stated in cabinet that Hellyer's recommendations would seriously annoy and disrupt the bureaucracy. The result was the shelving of excellent suggestions largely put together by the private sector. The bureaucrats, with an assist from one of their own in cabinet, carried the day.

Thirty years later, towards the end of the 1990s, I had another experience involving Sharp after meeting with the prime minister's chief of staff, Jean Pelletier. I had founded the non-profit Safety Sense Institute of Canada. Its principal mandate is to decrease death and injury from accidents. I had authored a number of safety family reference books which were endorsed and distributed by the American Trauma Society. Sharp was an advisor to the prime minister with an office down the hall from Chrétien in the East Block. Pelletier referred my dossier to Sharp. I met with him on a number of occasions, offering my services free of charge to government on matters of injury prevention. Ultimately, over lunch, Sharp informed me that he had talked with the prime minister and that my offer, most regretfully, had to be turned down. "Your initiative, Heward, would be most disturbing for the bureaucracy. That is my view and the prime minister concurs with it." Once more, Sharp and the bureaucrats got their way.

I believe these housing and safety proposals, with which I had first hand experience, are merely two of many examples of worthwhile private sector initiatives and suggestions being turned down.

When I became minister of science and technology in October 1979, I soon became aware of "my" bureaucrats' knee-jerk reactions to private sector suggestions: they were, invariably, victims of the "not-invented-here" syndrome. The civil servants felt that only their "made in the department" policy initiatives had any real validity. They protected their turf and turned down suggestions from outside with scorn. I did my best to put a halt to that in my department but, unfortunately, Canada still suffers from the "not-invented-here" attitude.

During World War II many able and loyal Canadians offered their services and expertise to the government in Ottawa and elsewhere. They were called "dollar-a-year men" and their patriotic dedication helped enormously to prosecute the war. A future prime minister and government must put an abrupt stop to the current "not-invented-here" attitude that dominates the Ottawa scene—where bureaucratic officials put up a Not Welcome sign to dedicated Canadians from the private sector. Dollar-a-year men should be encouraged to serve Canada in peacetime as they did in wartime. If our next prime minister and his cabinet officials encourage such an attitude, Canada will be the winner.

As the new parliament got underway in 1968, it seemed pretty much like business as usual. Trudeau's notion of participatory democracy seemed to constitute hype with no substance. Later on, Trudeaumania itself began to lose much of its lustre. Arrogance seemed the rule of the day. The prime minister gave the finger to western farmers, telling them they could sell their own wheat. No significant economic government legislation emerged from Trudeau's first full parliament. One Liberal minister allowed to me that things were difficult, as Lester Pearson had, in his view, completed most of the post-war agenda. The polls gave Stanfield and our party a good chance of taking over after the next elections. The imposition of the War Measures Act on October 15, 1970 buoyed the Liberals's chances for a short period of time. Many Canadians felt Trudeau acted as a fearless statesman, saving Canada and stamping out the forces of evil in my province. Hindsight and some revisionist thinking have cast doubts on the necessity for such harsh action. The recent publication of cabinet documents is most revealing in this regard. Many ministers felt sending in federal troops and the imposition of the War Measures Act was extreme overreaction.

During this period, I got to know Joe Clark very well, as he was a senior aide in Stanfield's office. We worked on one major project together. During my years out of the Commons, Frank Lowe of *Weekend Magazine* had commissioned me to write a number of cover stories for this weekly publication. I got to admire him and his editing skills immensely. One day, much to my surprise, Frank asked me to approach Stanfield to see if he would be willing to write a cover story spelling out his agenda and his priorities for action if he were to become prime minister. I had little doubt what his answer would be. A few days after Frank's request, I met with my leader in his office together with Joe Clark. Stanfield assigned Clark to work with me on the article. Joe did most of the work. During this time with Clark, I came to admire him and his sense of integrity and fun. Joe has a great sense of humour. *Weekend Magazine*, at that time, went into well over one million households from coast to coast. The article we put together was approved by the leader and proved to be most effective with *Weekend* readers.

As the 1972 elections approached, I had been working in my riding going door to door, day after day. By January 1972, I had completed over 18,000 home visits. I don't know what the state of our party's organization was like in the rest of Canada. In Quebec it was appalling and, in effect, non-existent. Jean-Jacques Bertrand and the Union Nationale had gone down in defeat to the Bourrassa Liberals in June 1970. Our provincial base had been weakened.

In December 1971, our party had its annual meeting in Ottawa. It was pretty much a routine affair. I visited Stanfield in his suite at the Château Laurier and remember John Fraser, a future MP from BC, being in the room with me. The state of the party in Quebec came up. I told Stanfield that if we started right away and concentrated on some winnable ridings, especially in rural and small-town Quebec, we could, with hard work, pick up ten seats. He looked disappointed and replied, "We can sweep Quebec. I want to recruit Claude Wagner as my lieutenant there." I was appalled. Wagner was a Liberal who had campaigned against us in the 1968 federal elections. He was never a team player in the Lesage government. Stanfield, a moderate centrist, did not seem to realize that Wagner was to the right of Genghis Khan. As a provincial judge, he won the label "the hanging judge." He gained this dubious distinction primarily from his conviction after the "Santa Claus" murder on the outskirts of Montreal. A gunman, disguised as Santa Claus, killed a Brink's guard. Wagner sentenced him to hang. When, before the 1970 provincial elections, he lost the leadership race to Robert Bourassa at the Montreal Forum, Wagner refused to approach the new leader and shake his hand. Bryce Mackasey, the federal member for Verdun, which included Wagner's provincial riding, had to forcibly drag him up on the stage to perform the traditional unity routine. When Wagner finally joined the PC Party, Mackasey said to me, "You guys can have him." Stanfield must have known of Wagner's right-wing views. He chose, to his later regret, to ignore them. This would prove to be a disaster and constituted Strike 2 for the man from Nova Scotia.

After the 1970 Liberal provincial leadership convention, Wagner had retired from active politics. Jean-Jacques Bertrand, then provincial premier, named him a provincial court judge. Bertrand, whose provincial riding was included within my federal riding, told me he appointed Wagner to the bench on the condition he would never enter active politics again. Did Stanfield know of Bertrand's conditions when he ultimately attempted to recruit Wagner? I leave this for the reader to judge. I have my own views on the subject.

In the spring of 1972, Stanfield was visiting the Eastern Townships and informed me outside the French TV Channel 7 in Sherbrooke that he had definitely decided to name Wagner. I was saddened. When the campaign got underway we had every reason to expect victory at the polls—there was even the possibility of our forming a majority government. But we conducted two campaigns, a national English campaign under Stanfield outside Quebec, and another completely separate campaign inside Quebec. All our Quebec advertising went under the slogan "Wagner—*c'est vrai.*"

The Wagner conversion cost the party $300,000 to set up a trust fund for him, thousands of dollars for his royal tour across the province, and an incredible amount directed into Ste-Hyacinthe-Bagot where Wagner would run after the resignation of the Honourable Théogène Ricard. Nothing was left over for other candidates in the province.

I started out the election campaign way ahead in my riding but even my militants were furious at the Wagner appointment. Some of my Union Nationale supporters were old time Blues who remembered Wagner's

Liberal campaign in the last provincial election. The pundits said that Brome-Missisquoi was the most likely riding in Quebec to go Progressive Conservative, and so the press invaded the riding as there had been national reports about my refusal to use the Wagner campaign material or to cooperate. My refusal to cooperate was based on my desire for political survival.

Toward the end of the campaign, when party headquarters in Ottawa realized that disaster was about to strike, they asked me to put the Wagner signs up. I still refused. During the last ten days of the campaign, after I'd shaken hands with the workers at the Dominion Textile Company in Magog, my agent was waiting for me with bad news. He informed me that party headquarters had put a stop payment on a $10,000 cheque he had in hand, which was meant to fulfill the party's pledge to me for the campaign. Brian Mulroney and the party elite in Montreal were playing hardball with me and my team. We really did not know what to do as there were bills to pay. This manoeuvre meant that on victory night, when I was elected with a resounding majority, we found ourselves $10,000 in debt. Wagner was the only other member elected in Quebec. He had just squeaked by in Ste-Hyacinthe-Bagot.

On the eve of the 1972 election, it seemed at one time that we were about to form a minority government. It was our cynical Quebec strategy that kept us out of power. Two weeks later at a service club meeting in Montreal, I was invited to sit at the head table with Stanfield, Wagner, and Senator Jacques Flynn. At a reception before the lunch, the party hierarchy studiously avoided me and Brian Mulroney expressed his annoyance to me. I was unhappy about his treatment, but I was entirely unprepared for what came next. Whether or not it was intentional I shall never know, but, in his introductory remarks, Stanfield said how pleased he was to be there with his "distinguished colleagues, Jacques Flynn and Claude Wagner." He then proceeded with his speech. Somebody from the back of the hall yelled out, "What about Grafftey?" He did not reply, and when the press corps surrounded Stanfield and myself at the end of the speech in order to get an explanation, Stanfield still didn't provide one. I returned to Knowlton more sad than angry. The Tories stayed in opposition for another seven years.

It will always be a mystery to me how a man such as Bob Stanfield ever went along with this outlandish scheme, which had been continually recommended to him by senior party organizers in Montreal. Had local candidates been encouraged and assisted in Quebec before and during that election, Bob Stanfield undoubtedly would have led us to power. Instead, the party leadership decided, with the help of a suitcase full of money, to metamorphose a "rouge" into a "bleu." On election day, the people of Quebec responded to this insult by overwhelmingly rejecting us at the polls. Trudeau formed an ill-deserved minority government. It was Strike 2 for Stanfield.

Wage and Price Controls — Strike 3

There was a feeling of frustration in our caucus after the 1972 elections. We were "so near but yet so far." On the other hand, I noticed a dangerous attitude surrounding the mindset of many of our MPs, including those in leadership roles. Somehow or other, many felt we would automatically come to power after the next election. Later on, this attitude would prove fatal to our chances.

Stanfield named me Opposition critic for the Secretary of State. Joe Clark proved to be the most effective and diligent member of my committee. He also, as a back bencher, seemed to catch the Speaker's eye on many occasions. During question period, his questions were both penetrating and to the point.

In mid-1973, Stanfield started to flirt with the idea of promoting wage and price controls—a sort of short-term pain for long-term gain idea. After Two Nations, and Wagner, wage and price controls would prove to be Strike 3 for Stanfield, ending his chances to move into 24 Sussex Drive.

The press and much of the public invariably admonish opposition parties to outline viable policy alternatives in order to demonstrate that they are capable of taking power in the future. It's obvious that the official opposition must have positive policy positions in place and be ready for their eventual "transition" to government. The press and public often tell opposition MPs that they are negative, always criticizing the government but never saying what they stand for. It is ironic that the same journalists who ask, "What do you stand for?" virtually ignore opposition spokesmen when they outline policy stances. Journalists feel that opposition parties, being in opposition, cannot bring into effect these policies and pay little or no attention to their policy declarations. For example, if an MP in opposition called a press conference to announce his or her party's stand on, let us say, pension legislation, he or she could expect only a small press turnout. On the other hand, if, in the House, he or she labelled the prime minister "the devil incarnate" on a quiet news day, they might even get a headline. Such is the Catch 22 situation for the opposition. The role of Her Majesty's Loyal Opposition is to shine light on the weakness of government performance and legislation. Invariably, the government says all is white, the Opposition says all is black, and the public choose their shade of grey.

In effect, in Canada and, I expect, in most other democratic countries, governments defeat themselves. The public rarely, if ever, vote opposition parties in. They vote governments out.

The Progressive Conservative Party in Quebec

In 1935, in the city of Sherbrooke, Quebec, Maurice Duplessis was the prime mover in founding the Union Nationale Party. This party was a coalition of discontented Liberals and Conservatives. Within a year, the Liberals would jump ship and leave the newly-formed coalition, which would become a nationalist conservative force in my province. Soon, Duplessis would become premier, governing Quebec with an iron fist. With the exception of the World War II years, when the Liberal Adélard Godbout held the reins of power, Duplessis would reign supreme until his sudden death in 1959.

The Union Nationale, under Duplessis, while nominally conservative "bleu," were historically lukewarm to my party. Mackenzie King's divide-and-rule policy of "conscription if necessary, but not necessarily conscription" played its part. How often did I hear loud debates in our living room involving my father. He had deep roots in Quebec and, together with his friends, detested King for what they called his divide-and-rule pussyfooting. On the other side, King's Liberal supporters said King kept the country united during wartime years.

When Louis St-Laurent took over from King, there was no way Duplessis would oppose the popular Liberal francophone prime minister while St-Laurent had the unilingual Colonel George Drew, our party leader, confronting him from the Opposition benches. It was not until St-Laurent resigned in 1957, after his defeat, and Lester Pearson took over for the Grits that Duplessis opened his purse strings for the Tories. In the 1958 elections he set his troops free to support us. Still, we were not putting down real roots in Quebec.

Where were the Conservatives in Quebec during this time? The answer to this is, they opted out of all meaningful activity in my province, leaving the field open to the pro-federalist Liberals and eventually the separatist Parti Québécois. The die was cast, with the ultimate disastrous results for my party and, in my view, for Canada.

During the federal elections of 1972, I remember shaking hands early one morning with a young voter at his factory gate in Farnham, Quebec. He said, "Grafftey, your party is organized at the provincial level in every province except Quebec. Are you the party of the English?" What could I say?

The defeat of the Union Nationale under Jean-Jacques Bertrand in 1970 by the Bourrassa Liberals spelled the end of the party of Duplessis.

Once re-elected to the Commons in 1972, I became a strong advocate for a provincial Progressive Conservative Party in Quebec. In the winter of 1973, I organized a large dinner in Sherbrooke. Hundreds attended, from every corner of the province. The purpose of the meeting was to get the ball rolling to establish our party at the provincial level. Bob Stanfield attended the dinner and was the guest speaker, but he turned thumbs down on the initiative, on the advice of Mulroney and his entourage. The latter believed in organization from the top down and had little regard for grass roots organization at the constituency level. This was, in my view, a major error of political judgement on the part of Stanfield.

By the winter of 1973, it became apparent to me that Stanfield would adopt wage and price controls as his number one policy plank. I doubt if most caucus members understood the implications of such a move, political or otherwise. We were behaving as if we were already in power. When the election of 1974 was finally called, our wage and price control policy was all I heard about from the voters. Trudeau and the Grits went on the attack telling workers, among other things, that the Tories would freeze their wages. In mid-election, Trudeau visited Cowansville in the centre of my riding. He spoke with a loudspeaker in front of the Town Hall where a large crowd, including many workers, were gathered. I parked my car nearby in order to listen. Trudeau said, "I know Heward Grafftey has been a good member. I admit that, but he supports a Party that wants to freeze your wages." "Zap—you're frozen" shouted a band of Liberal supporters from the crowd. During the election, I had a distinctly uneasy feeling. We were on the defensive and the Grits on the attack. It seemed that we were the Government, and the Grits the Opposition, instead of vice-versa. On election day, July 8, 1974, I increased my majority by a substantial margin. Wagner was the only other Quebec Tory elected. Trudeau formed another majority government.

Once more, the party had been severely wounded and after Strike 3, the writing was on the wall for Stanfield.

CHAPTER FOUR

Clark to Mulroney

Stanfield's lack of electoral success, coupled with growing unrest within the party caucus, prompted him to call it quits. A leadership convention was called for February 1976. It was to be held in Ottawa.

The 1976 Conservative leadership convention was a study in contrasts. This time, the right wing was led by Diefenbaker, a reversal of the position he held in 1967. The left wing (the so-called Red Tories) was led by Stanfield. There were a number of candidates on each side. Jack Horner, Paul Hellyer, Claude Wagner, Sinclair Stevens, and Pat Nowlan were on the right, and Jim Gillies, Flora MacDonald, John Fraser, and Joe Clark represented the left wing of the party. It was difficult to know where Mulroney stood.

The convention was a contrast of styles as well as policies. Sinclair Stevens, Claude Wagner, and Brian Mulroney ran expensive campaigns, with some of the money going towards big-name entertainment, refreshments, meals, and delegate accommodation. Mulroney, especially, stood out in this area. Although he has steadfastly refused to divulge any details concerning the financial resources behind his first leadership run, people knowledgeable in such matters have estimated his disbursements at $300,000 or more. That Mulroney finished the race without a deficit is a testimony to his fundraising ability.

Clark's victory on the fourth ballot was a surprise to many. He was immediately labeled "Joe Who?"—a catchy phrase that would haunt him even after he became prime minister. However, Clark was not a political neophyte. He had served as MP for about three years before the leadership race and had occupied a number of important positions within the party organization. In Alberta, he worked as principal speech writer in 1959 for Cam Kirby, the leader of the provincial Progressive Conservatives, and he helped put together Peter Lougheed's winning leadership campaign for the Alberta PCs. He was PC National Youth Federation president and worked at PC national headquarters in 1962, helping to put the election team together. In 1967, Clark helped run Davie Fulton's leadership bid. Following that convention, Clark was asked to join the staff of Robert Stanfield's office, where he remained until 1972, when he returned to Alberta to plan his bid for the riding of Rocky Mountain, which elected him in that year.

Clark began considering a run for the leadership following his win in the 1974 election. He began scouring the country for possible supporters. Like other candidates for the leadership, he realized that Stanfield would step down before long. As early as December 1974, Clark began meeting with friends and key party insiders, trying to determine whether he had a base of support. Financial considerations were also a determining factor in whether Clark would run. The 1967 PC leadership convention had been one of the most expensive in Canadian history, with more delegates assembling than ever before. Indications were that the 1976 convention would be equally expensive, in part because of the increasing reliance on media and travel during the campaign. Since 1967, the nature of running for a party leadership has taken on the appearance and methods of a mini-presidential race, complete with whistle-stop swings through virtually every important riding in the country. Clark, who had just acquired a new home in the affluent Rockliffe area of Ottawa, could not inject much money himself into the race, nor could he count on financial support from the business community; that support would go to the other candidates in the race, especially to Brian Mulroney. If Clark were to run, he would have to run a low-key, frugal campaign, in the age of mega-dollar politics.

Having received the assurance that his former boss, Peter Lougheed, would not enter the leadership race, Clark tossed his hat into the ring, a novice MP from Alberta doing battle with the party's eastern elite. Some of his advisors considered that a third- or fourth-place finish would be good for Clark's career, possibly leading to a major cabinet post if he threw his support behind the victorious candidate. Clark's main opposition would come from Flora MacDonald, whose ideological stance was similar to Clark's. MacDonald's personality and charisma—which drew a large number of people—would hamper Clark, who lacked a distinctive style.

The Clark team waited until four weeks before the convention before investing in campaign posters, banners, and related materials. Meanwhile, other candidates were traveling the country in fully decked-out buses and appearing on television with a backdrop of campaign posters. In their attempt to run a low-key campaign, the Clark forces were in fact underselling their candidate. In any other circumstances, such strategic miscalculations would most likely have been fatal to his leadership bid.

At the official start of the leadership race, all the candidates were asked to submit detailed financial reports to the PC national executive. These reports highlight the frugality of Clark's campaign. At one point his campaign was so strapped for cash that some of Clark's close friends and associates had to co-sign a letter of credit for $20,000 before funds could be borrowed privately.

Aided by some favourable media coverage, however, Clark's campaign took off in the closing weeks of the race. The mood of the convention was decidedly right of centre. Polls taken at the convention showed that a majority of the delegates described themselves as conservative and on the right of the spectrum, while a very small percentage perceived themselves as liberal in areas such as social spending.

The main challengers for the leadership were a varied group. Paul Hellyer was supported by at least twenty Tory MPs, as well as the Diefenbaker wing of the party. His main selling point was his parliamentary experience, and his discourse was hard-right. Jack Horner's campaign was personality oriented. He also occupied the right of the spectrum, but his rhetoric frightened some delegates as it was perceived as too strong. Horner forces were largely based in the West and did not seem inclined to make inroads with the party's eastern elite, essential to emerge victorious. The Wagner team was also on the right of the spectrum and was perhaps the most secretive of the leadership campaigns. There was little to be learned from his campaign organizers, and throughout the campaign the former "hanging judge" remained vague in his policy pronouncements.

Mulroney's campaign was also soft on policy, but it was big on show. The Mulroney team sold the person rather than the program. Mulroney, having no political experience as an elected representative, was virtually unknown to those outside the party. Therefore, Mulroney's team set out to create a public profile, an operation that had a $300,000 price tag. In the end the Mulroney strategy backfired, as delegates began questioning the substance behind the PR packaging.

The remainder of the field was split among a number of lesser-known candidates who either couldn't raise the funds for a strong campaign or had support that was too local or regional to appeal to a wide number of delegates from across the country.

By convention week, Clark had managed to raise his profile substantially, but now came the crucial stage. His campaign was again cash poor at the precise time when mounting the final convention assault would require large infusions of money. Hotel rooms and office space had been booked, and money would have to be found to pay for them. Clark found himself trapped by his own strategy. He had run a low-key campaign, and his resulting low profile meant that he did not gather the exposure Mulroney and Horner had. Delegates would be unable to gauge his possible strength at the convention and might therefore be reluctant to contribute to his campaign. Clark's campaign had to borrow the funds to stage a final convention blitz. Clark had entered the campaign with a pledge to spend only what he could raise. To keep that pledge, borrowed funds would have to be repaid by the convention's end. Faced with this situation, the Clark campaign organized a nationwide telephone blitz in the last week before the convention. The phone drive netted enough to pay off all outstanding bills and loans. Clark's frugal campaign cost $169,135, most of which had been raised through small, individual contributions of approximately $150.

One aspect of financing greatly concerned me during the leadership campaign. Under the Elections Act, individuals can contribute to party constituency associations and receive receipts for income tax purposes. It is obvious to me that the intent of the act meant that monies so raised were to be directed towards constituency activities. Many leadership candidates raised money for their campaigns through their riding associations and give contributors receipts for income tax purposes. Surely this practice is a case for reform.

The candidates would be able to gauge their support on the first night of the convention, when all the delegates gathered at the Ottawa Civic Centre. When the candidates were introduced, Clark received a strong ovation, but so did his main opponents. The delegate-tracking system that the Clark team had devised began to fall apart, making it impossible for Clark to find out which way some of the undecided delegates were going.

But who exactly were these delegates? As with the 1967 PC leadership convention, a disproportionate number of the 1976 delegates represented the professional elite of Canadian society. The working class was under-represented, as usual. The majority of the delegates had post-secondary education and incomes above the national average. Homemakers were few in number and did not represent a cohesive voting block. In addition, as in all previous conventions, the ex officio contingent was dispro-portionately large, this time representing over 25% of the delegates. The one major difference from the 1967 convention was that in 1976 most Quebec delegates had been selected at the riding level, rather than being blow-in delegates. The presence of two strong candidates from Quebec, Mulroney and Wagner, probably explains this. Many of these Quebec delegates were chosen as parts of slates organized by the Wagner and, to a lesser extent, the Mulroney forces.

Friday, February 20, day two of the convention, was the day for policy sessions—a chance for delegates to question the leadership candidates. Many questions were planted to make one candidate look good or an opposing candidate look bad. Overall, Clark did well in the policy forums, although Brian Mulroney was also well received, especially with his positive stance on bilingualism.

Saturday was the crucial day of the convention, the day of the candidate speeches. Clark's team had arranged for his speech to be introduced by Allan Laakkonen, a grassroots party worker. Laakkonen's speech began with his introducing himself as the "one who rings the doorbells ... works the committee rooms ... and carries the signs." Clark thereby enhanced his populist image while the other delegates only emphasized their associations with the back-room elite by relying on introductions from the Conservative party's establishment. In the draw that allocated the order of the speeches, Clark came out fifth, a good position in the middle of the pack. He would speak after MacDonald, but before such main-line candidates as Hellyer and Wagner.

Clark entered the Civic Centre arena on Saturday afternoon in an antique landau as his campaign's brass band played the campaign's theme song. The whole effect was one of sleekness, an effort to show that if they chose to, the Clark team could outperform the Mulroney forces at their own game. Clark's speech, however, did not go well; it was too long and it lacked excitement. To make things worse, Wagner and MacDonald spoke compellingly.

Clark's speech had been geared towards raising support among the Quebec delegates, and to this end, a fair portion of it was delivered in French. This effort would reduce his image as a Western anglophone and place him among the bilingual candidates—Mulroney and Wagner. By emphasizing his bilingual aspect, Clark hoped to be perceived as a possible winner in the next federal election where the party would need the Quebec vote to win.

Sunday was voting day. The first ballot's results would finally settle the question of the accuracy of the delegate tracking that all the campaigns had been running throughout the race. The Clark team was expecting 300 votes on the first ballot, and when the results were announced and he had only 277, many in his camp thought it was all over. However, Clark had expected fourth place on the first ballot and he found himself third. He was the leading candidate from outside Quebec. The somber mood in the Clark camp changed as delegates began moving to his section in the Civic Centre. First, James Gillies potentially added 120 votes to Clark's total for the second ballot. Then, to everyone's surprise, Sinclair Stevens pledged his support for Clark, adding a potential 182 votes. Stevens had been identified with the right wing of the party, and his support for Clark was a turning point. If Stevens could support Clark, then a number of other right-of-centre delegates could consider Clark as the best alternative candidate around whom to build a coalition of the various party factions for the next election.

The second-ballot results had Clark second only to Wagner. Clark received 532 votes, Wagner 667. Mulroney finished third, with 419 votes. The next round of withdrawals would be critical. As expected, MacDonald made her way to Clark's box, while Horner was moving over to Wagner's box. Mulroney was positive that there would be a fourth ballot and chose to stay in for the third. Either way, his support would have sealed the convention's conclusions.

The third-ballot results still had Clark second to Wagner, 969 to 1,003, with Mulroney losing support and dropping to 369.

Mulroney elected to stay in for the fourth ballot. He had no chance of victory but was not damaging his position within the party by siding with one or the other of his opponents. Despite this, many of Mulroney's supporters went over to Clark. Ideologically, they were closer to Clark than to Wagner.

Clark's team knew they had won by the looks on the faces of Claude Wagner and his wife. The results had been leaked to them, and their downcast expressions said it all. Clark, who had been working on his victory speech (he had never made allowances for defeat), was cheered loudly when the results were announced. He had won by 65 votes, one of the smallest margins of victory ever.

The Fall of Clark and the Rise of Mulroney

Although Joe Clark is again leading the PC Party as I write in 2002, his election as leader in 1976 seemed to have within it the seeds of its own destruction.

Between 1958 and 1962, while John Diefenbaker presided over a majority Progressive Conservative government, a number of bright young people who would play important roles in Canada were drawn to Ottawa. I have a clear recollection of some of the assistants who worked in ministers' offices, including Michael Pitfield and Marc Lalonde, who came to help Justice Minister David Fulton. There was Brian Mulroney, a student at that time, who worked in the office of Alvin Hamilton, then minister of agriculture, as a special assistant. I also remember many visits to the Hill by Joe Clark, who was then active with the Young Conservatives. Little did I realize at the time that I was meeting a future clerk of the Privy Council, a future minister of finance, and two future prime ministers.

During the 1962 federal election campaign, Alvin Hamilton visited my home riding to address a group of English-speaking farmers. His young assistant accompanied him. Mulroney must have circulated among the constituents that evening, because I have in my files a letter that he wrote to one of them. The letter seems to show potential for public service—a readiness to respond to an individual's needs and to provide whatever service or information his access to ministry resources could.

Despite the ability he might have had for serving and charming constituents, Mulroney did not do most of his party work at the grass roots level. At a very young age, he had the ear of Diefenbaker. He would later establish equally good relations with Stanfield. His particular service to the party was most often rendered through his skill at fundraising activities. He played a major part in organizing fundraising dinners for the party in Montreal at regular intervals. This work undoubtedly served his career by bringing him into contact with corporate leaders.

Because of the influence they would have on Mulroney's career, the character of the old-guard Montreal Tory establishment to which some of those corporate leaders belonged is important to consider. Even though our party was officially named the Progressive Conservative Party in 1942 in order to accommodate John Bracken and the Western Progressive Movement, many old-time, right-wing Tories never took the "Progressive" label very seriously. When the premier of Ontario, George Drew, became national party leader in 1948, the party truly took on an added conservative flavour. At that time, the Progressive Conservative Party was virtually non-existent in Quebec, except for a few Tories among the Montreal establishment who had to be seen to be believed. One of them said to me in that period that they might have nominated Diefenbaker because of his fighting qualities, but the name "Diefenbaker" would never do. Only upon Drew's imminent retirement did I consider joining a party that I felt could be uniquely Canadian in being *progressive*, civilized, decent, and humane in social policy, while simultaneously, feeling that if we could transform the traditional Tory party along those lines, we could widen its electoral appeal and credibility. For me, there has never been any inconsistency in being progressive in social policy and conservative in economic policy. The two notions are in no way mutually exclusive, as liberals and socialists would have us believe.

When Mulroney and I first met, we were approaching the political process from different directions. Mulroney was making his first moves to get onside with the Montreal Tories. I was putting down roots in a rural, small-town, largely francophone riding across the St. Lawrence River from Montreal. While it was just a few miles away from the city, my riding was in another world from that inhabited by the people Mulroney was cultivating in Montreal. One acquaintance in the city's Tory circles pleaded with me to run in "an important West Island riding," as opposed to getting lost in the hinterland.

I felt that Mulroney had a certain detachment. He seemed to scorn day-to-day political work at the constituency level and workers who toiled in those fields. He and his friends were tacticians, officers who directed the efforts of lower-ranking workers. By the time I was named minister of state for social programs in 1979, I was publicly critical of the Montreal party generals. Mulroney was aware of my criticisms, but hardly abashed by them.

Elected representatives were held in such low regard by this group that we were sometimes forgotten altogether. Mulroney and his friends arranged a fundraising dinner at the Queen Elizabeth Hotel some months before the 1979 election. A number of speeches and activities had been organized, but Roch LaSalle and I, the only two elected representatives from the Province of Quebec, were overlooked. Only after intervention from people of Clark's group did Brian arrange to have us introduced to the audience at an appropriate time.

For the past couple of decades, the roles of the party caucus and elected members of Parliament have diminished in direct proportion to the rise in power of the extra-parliamentary wing of the party. In the television age, the longer elected officials remain elected, the more negative baggage they normally accumulate. Mulroney would later capitalize on this unfortunate phenomenon in a city where there were no elected Progressive Conservative members and where the party power brokers never attempted to conceal their contempt for those who managed to get elected. I was not always faking when I quipped that my greatest sin against the party establishment in Quebec was that I got elected.

Mulroney and his group showed little sign of their later ability to sweep Quebec during the Clark years.

The time span between the convention in February 1976 and the election of 1979 should have been a period of rebuilding for the Conservatives in Quebec, but it was not. At the convention, Clark had received more support from Quebec than any of the other candidates from outside the province. Clark's view of the country and his stand on major issues should have been acceptable to most Quebecers. The constitutional debate had become polarized between the separatist option of René Lévesque and Trudeau's total faith in centralized federal authority. Like Trudeau's colleague and old friend Gérard Pelletier, Clark articulated an acceptable and viable middle option between the two constitutional extremes.

I believe Clark's lack of success in Quebec was partly attributable to the paucity of cooperation from the Mulroney and Wagner camps. Never a team player, Wagner treated his younger leader with haughty indifference. Realizing that Clark would not repeat Stanfield's mistake of appointing a Quebec lieutenant, Wagner was ripe for picking by the Liberals. When Trudeau tempted him with an offer, Wagner was quick to swallow the bait. While Trudeau gave Jack Horner a cabinet post to lure him across the floor, he could hardly do the same for Wagner because Wagner had already switched parties once in recent history. The solution that Trudeau found to get Wagner out of his seat in the Commons was to appoint him to the Senate.

Trudeau was using the tools he had available to try to eliminate PC representation from the political map of Quebec. A number of his emissaries came to visit me in my West Block office, ostensibly for a friendly chat, but more precisely to see if, after twenty years of hard fighting, I wouldn't welcome a comfortable seat in the Red Chamber. They soon got my answer. It was an emphatic no.

In all fairness, I did find the Senate useful on at least one occasion during my parliamentary career. When attending the United Nations as a delegate in 1958, I wanted to see the New York Yankees play in the World Series. This desire prompted me to write a letter on Commons stationery to the Yankees' front office, asking for Series tickets. Ten days went by, and I had no answer. I was about to give up when I got a brain wave. Senators are powerful and important people in the United States. It came to mind that officials at the Yankees' front office would not differentiate between the importance of senators on this and on the other side of the border. So I dictated a letter, this time on Senate stationery, and had a reluctant senator sign it. The letter was delivered by courier, and the very next day a messenger arrived with the tickets. The only problem was, the senator decided that he wanted some of them. I got to keep the rest.

During Clark's early stewardship of the party, Mulroney sulked conspicuously on the sidelines. One indication of this involved a meeting Clark convened in the leader's boardroom in the Centre Block of the Parliament Buildings, soon after his nomination as leader. The purpose of the meeting was to arrange a formula whereby the national party would assist defeated leadership candidates to meet their campaign deficits. All candidates had agreed to disclose the sources of their funds in an open and honest way. Mulroney did not turn up at the meeting and refused to disclose the source of his funds.

In the election run-up two years later, a *Financial Post* article appeared that quoted Mulroney as saying, "If Joe Clark wins this election, I'll eat this plate. I mean, let's look at it. Can you see any way he can win? Any way at all?" Mulroney was confident that he could provide the party with the kind of leadership that would be much more attractive to voters. He did not run in the 1979 election.

At a caucus meeting following the publication of the article, several MPs referred to it. I warned Clark that he would face the same fate that had overtaken Diefenbaker and Stanfield if he didn't publicly demand party loyalty and discipline. Clark just asked us to keep our cool and expressed no public annoyance at Mulroney. I have always felt that he was, and still is, spooked by Mulroney.

While we went on to form a minority government after the 1979 campaign, once again the party was routed in Quebec. Joe was doing his best, but he had elected to work with the same old gang, and they had produced the same old results.

We might have done better. Trudeau was more popular than the Liberal Party, but many people voted for the leader, not the party. Still, a strong grassroots campaign might have changed the results in some ridings. Instead, some Montreal organizer took a totally inexplicable tack. He leaked to the press a list of ridings the party had written off as hopeless —ridings where sincere candidates were working long hours to break through the Liberals' thick red line.

Then there was the province-wide ad campaign. As the election campaign drew to a close, somebody dreamed up the idea of a TV spot ad showing Trudeau in prison, with his hands gripping the bars. A loud voice-over cited all the crimes of the Liberal government, and the prime minister was pronounced *coupable*—guilty. Even party supporters angrily denounced the advertisement as being not only negative but in extremely poor taste.

Election day showed that the Quebec team had let the party down again. It was a minority government. With a reasonable showing in Quebec, Clark could have formed a majority government and be able to name more cabinet ministers from Quebec. I was one of the two members elected from Quebec. As I was walking up the driveway towards the Governor General's residence for the swearing-in, I was greeted by Pierre Trudeau at the front door. He was about to drive away in his convertible sportscar with the top down. He greeted me enthusiastically and said, "Congratulations, Heward. You richly deserve it." Pierre and his cabinet had just seen the Governor General for the last time. I had won my own riding with a comfortable majority and was sworn in as minister of state for social programs. We were painfully aware of how under-represented we were in this politically crucial province. Trudeau had used patronage appointments very effectively in promoting his political objectives. It is now common knowledge that Clark had little interest in the discretionary patronage appointments that were in his power to disperse. There was the case of Guy Charbonneau, a Montreal insurance broker who had done an excellent job as a fundraiser in Quebec. Clark did not consider this an adequate reason to appoint Charbonneau to the Canadian Senate, but Mulroney and his associates read the riot act and the appointment went through.

Quebec patronage appointments continued to be an issue between Joe Clark and the Quebec party organization. It surfaced late in the summer of 1979 at a cabinet meeting at the Château Frontenac in Quebec City. We had long and good working sessions. Whoever believes the "wimp" label that is sometimes hung on Clark has not witnessed his solid and creative handling of cabinet. On the last day of the meetings, we were informed that the Quebec City regional organization had prepared a luncheon for us. We were to find that the lunch was bait for an ambush.

Clark had neglected to make any significant discretionary appointments, except for Senator Arthur Tremblay, who had been a senior provincial mandarin during the Lesage years. Daniel Johnson and his followers had long called for Tremblay's head, but to no avail. Joe was apparently impressed, not by his service to the blue machine, but by his credentials as a constitutional expert. I have often met people with strong points of view on our Canadian constitution, but I'm not sure how one defines an expert in that field. The boys from Quebec were not looking for that kind of qualification for patronage appointments. At the luncheon, they attacked Clark's lack of support for their efforts. Clark sat red-faced. His handling of patronage matters, distasteful as they were to him, proved to be a large part of Clark's undoing. "To the victors belong the spoils" didn't play well as a tune in the Clark repertoire.

During nine months in office, Clark made only approximately 150

Tory appointments—ten were senators. When the Clark government fell in December 1979, a list of 153 appointments was awaiting approval. Clark said they were meant to be Christmas presents, but now they were frozen because of defeat. Mulroney would eventually profit from this state of affairs, as he had a more pragmatic attitude to the use of rewards and would exploit it to the full. During his climb to the leadership in 1983, he pulled out all the stops on the issue and severely wounded Clark by making it abundantly clear that a Mulroney-led government would look after the faithful.

While Clark is, in so many ways, warm, civilized, and sincere, I felt he had an innate shyness that discouraged him from reaching out to stroke his supporters. Stroking and keeping in touch with the faithful are critically important in politics, and Clark largely neglected this important part of his role. A phone call, letter, or pat on the back from a party leader can keep party workers enthusiastic. Politicians and political workers need recognition and encouragement. Long periods of silence from the leader lower morale. Clark was guilty of omission in this area. Mulroney, like former president Lyndon Johnson, was a telephone junkie.

The summer months of 1979 skipped by before we knew it. There was loud press and public criticism over the fact that we had gone through the summer without facing Parliament and convening the House. Clark and his ministers were getting their feet under their desks. With the exception of the Diefenbaker interlude, the Grits had been in power for almost forty years. Much work was to be done. While our transition to power was better than during the Diefenbaker years, it wasn't easy, and as we made our plans to meet Parliament, there were few concrete results for people to see. I knew that we needed a more substantial legislative agenda.

Before the House was convened in October of 1979, an event took place that should have been cause for concern and should have forewarned cabinet ministers and members of our caucus. Clark announced, without cabinet consultation, the government's desire to move our embassy in Israel from Tel Aviv to Jerusalem. The political storm over this dubious decision caused an uproar. Clark then assigned Robert Stanfield to visit the Middle East in order to investigate the advisability of such a move. Stanfield returned to Canada advising strongly against Clark's hastily proposed initiative. Clark did an about-face and withdrew his proposal. Enough said.

On August 16, 1979, John Diefenbaker died suddenly. I walked with Pierre Trudeau in the funeral cortege between Parliament Hill and the Anglican cathedral. I was not surprised at Diefenbaker's funeral. It was not totally unlike the rites for Winston Churchill at Saint Paul's in London. The Dief had had a hand in the preparations for his spectacular sendoff. After Lester Pearson's funeral in Ottawa somebody remarked to Diefenbaker "Wasn't it a lovely service!" "Wait till you see mine," quipped the Dief. After Diefenbaker's funeral I stood on the station platform beside Bunny Pound, his faithful and loyal secretary for many years, as the private train bearing his body pulled out on its journey west to Saskatchewan.

While Clark's handling of his cabinet and government matters in general must be given high marks, he had flaws that would prove fatal. What happened next would soon open the door for Mulroney and his supporters. Each morning the prime minister would meet with his non-elected staff, much as does the president of the United States. Often, to the resentment of able elected cabinet officers, these people started to wield enormous power and influence. Henry Kissinger wrote of his White House years that frequently those who had helped the president get elected were the least equipped to help him govern. Likewise, Joe's non-elected advisers were about to get him into trouble.

Two major events helped cripple the Clark government, orchestrating its fall in the House and the ultimate defeat at the polls in February of 1980. They were the attempted privatization of Petro-Canada and the eighteen-cent tax on gas at the pumps. Cabinet briefings on Petro-Canada and proposed privatization reminded me of *Alice's Adventures in Wonderland*.

Sometimes when we listen to modern contemporary music, look at modern art, or hear readings of modern poetry, we pretend to appreciate and understand these offerings at first exposure. I well remember attending symphony concerts when a contemporary piece was played for the first time. At intermission, the audience would gather in the lobby. "How did you like it?" one listener would ask another. "Oh, I found it very interesting!" would be a normal reply. Interesting was one thing. Understanding, love, and, appreciation would only come after repeated listening.

Cabinet briefings on Petro-Canada by the bureaucracy reminded me of looking at abstract art for the very first time. Reserving judgement in the hope of future understanding and appreciation was the order of the day. Bureaucratic gobbledegook and flow charts left me dazed. When the cabinet broke for refreshment breaks during the briefing, everybody feigned interest, but nobody pretended to understand the implications of the convoluted presentation by officials from Energy, Mines and Resources. In the end, Clark virtually became his own energy minister, while officials in the department remained in their exotic dream world. Soon he would be in open warfare with Peter Lougheed, the premier of Alberta, over an energy policy that in effect never really got off the drawing board. We were to blame, but ministers found it impossible to defend a policy when departmental briefings were so horrendously deficient and overly complicated. The Government was wounded.

The next crisis was precipitated by John Crosbie, then minister of finance. Brilliant as he was, he was also proud and stubborn. Because of budget secrecy, cabinet ministers were not aware of the budget provisions. We should have seen the problems in the provision to tax gas eighteen cents per gallon at the pump. Crosbie was about to play Russian roulette with the government's future. His promotion of short-term pain for long-term gain constituted an act of political masochism. We were in trouble before we knew it.

On the morning of December 14, 1979, after a motion was moved by Bob Rae of the NDP, my executive assistant Brian Derrick informed me that there was a strong rumour on Parliament Hill that the combined opposition would attempt to defeat us on a vote of non-confidence that evening. By that time, I knew we were in trouble as the political implications of the eighteen-cent gas increase were hitting us, but I felt little need to worry. Surely Clark would act and enable us to survive, even if we were in a minority situation.

Clark could have saved the day had he wanted to. He didn't make that effort. It is reported that the leadership qualities Clark displayed with his cabinet colleagues at the cabinet table were lacking during the meetings with non-elected officials. He had often seemed lost, as he found it hard to sort out the issues. How else can we explain what happened the next day?

Clark's non-elected advisers didn't believe the opposition would go to the limit in the House to defeat us. Clark had seriously under-estimated the cunning, intrigue, and ability of the Liberal House Leader, Allan MacEachen. After all, Trudeau had announced his retirement and merely sat like a bearded ghost in the Commons, refusing to carry out his constitutional duties as Opposition leader. While dissolving the House and calling an election are solely the responsibility of the prime minister, I assumed Clark would sound out his cabinet colleagues on this issue. My assumption was wrong. He chose to closet himself with the non-elected officials, completely detached from the realities of grassroots public opinion. They compared circumstances at that time with those surrounding the Diefenbaker minority government when it went to the people in 1958. The move had worked well for Diefenbaker, but our situation was different. The comparison was seriously flawed.

We had no legislative record to go to the people with, as had Diefenbaker twenty-two years before when he dissolved the House and let his minority government face the people. Diefenbaker had been far ahead in the polls with an excellent minority-government legislative agenda already completed. We had, in December 1979, completed no such agenda and were more than 10% behind in the polls. Diefenbaker was in control of the House and dissolved it. Clark, as prime minister, would be forced into an election after being defeated in the House.

There was an additional factor that influenced Clark's judgement. The prime minister realized that many tough economic decisions would have to be made by the Government and felt that cooperating with the NDP in a minority situation would be futile. He *wanted* to clear the air and go to the people. It was in this spirit that he entered the House at eight that evening. All of his cabinet colleagues were in the dark, and by the time the House convened, we were individually and collectively concerned, gathering and talking in small groups on the floor of the House. The prime minister just sat in his seat, seemingly unperturbed by it all. As is the custom before all votes, the Whip gave Walter Baker, our House leader, the head count. We were going down. There weren't enough PCs present for the vote. Baker had done his job as best he could. The press later contrived to blame Baker directly or indirectly for the ensuing calamity, but he was merely the messenger, and I assume his message was delivered. It was still not too late to act. The prime minister could have had his House leader announce a change in the order of House business to permit us to gather our forces and postpone the vote.

Clark did not act to save the government. The bells stopped ringing. The vote was taken. We went down to defeat on prime-time television before an incredulous public. Clark dissolved the House and went to the people. Clark and his advisers felt the public would bury the Liberals on election day for forcing an election. That sentiment did, in fact, last for a while early on in the campaign, but soon public opinion turned against a government that had held power but allowed a weak and rudderless opposition to force them into an election.

At a recent fundraising dinner in Toronto I had a long chat with the former premier of Ontario, Bill Davis. Davis informed me that after our defeat that night in the House in 1979, he attempted to convince Clark to rearrange the Commons' order paper the next day by putting other legislative matters on the agenda thus avoiding the necessity of going to the people. Davis's efforts were to no avail. Clark would not listen. He believed he could win a majority mandate.

As Clark's grip gradually slipped—first by losing in the 1980 general election in March, and then by capitulating at the party meeting in Winnipeg after nearly 70% of those attending the meeting voted to endorse his leadership—the stage was set for Mulroney. The fact that he had never held an elective office would count for little as long as there were no truly democratic rules in place regarding leadership funding and leadership-convention delegate selection. A sizeable section of the parliamentary caucus had swung against Clark. By the winter of 1983, most of the power and influence rested with the extra-parliamentary wing of the party. This was Mulroney's base of power. Added to that, Mulroney had long since had his hands on important segments of the party fundraising apparatus. Lots of money would be at his disposal.

Mulroney's rise to power at the Ottawa convention in June 1983 is based on a number of factors. There was the increasing power of the extra-parliamentary membership itself. Mulroney's initial power base was in the city of Montreal, where there were no Progressive Conservative Members of Parliament. The coterie of establishment party people that surrounded Mulroney capitalized on this and helped mobilize anti-Clark sentiment. Then there was the phenomenon of "anybody but Clark." Although Clark received support at the party's annual meeting in Ottawa, he was still having a great deal of trouble leading the caucus, and a substantial and growing number within the caucus were dissatisfied with his leadership.

Some of Mulroney's backers tried to get Clark to call a leadership contest after the 1981 party general meeting in Ottawa, where he received 66.4% of the vote. Clark refused, realizing that he had two years to go and that a large proportion of the vote against him hinged on the fact that he had recently lost power and that he had let his minority government fall.

The two years after the 1981 general meeting in Ottawa were filled with frenzied activity on the part of Mulroney supporters. It seemed that the Ritz Carlton Hotel in Montreal, of which Mulroney was a director, became the unofficial headquarters for his leadership campaign. The hotel was situated a stone's throw away from Mulroney's office as president and chief executive officer of the Iron Ore Company of Canada. Had Joe Clark opted to keep in touch with some of his closest friends and supporters, he would have been aware of what was going on. Perhaps, deep down, he was, but if so, he made an odd decision when he agreed to meet with Mulroney at the Ritz Carlton on December 6, 1982, not much over a month before the next general party meeting was to be held in Winnipeg. As I watched the TV reporting that day, I felt sick. There was poor Joe, crowded into a room at the Ritz beside Mulroney. The room was jammed full of Mulroney's supporters. While I looked at the television, I saw Mulroney put his arm on Joe's shoulder as he said, "He's my leader. He always will be." I was perfectly aware that the Mulroney forces were out, with plenty of cash, establishing their plans to overthrow Clark once the Winnipeg convention got underway. Mulroney knew it too, and to see Joe there, in enemy territory, supposedly believing Mulroney's pledge of allegiance, was painful to me.

Later, at a weekend meeting of the Quebec party, national president Peter Blaikie had a confrontation with the Mulroney supporters. He was upset that they were attempting to take control of the party in Quebec. In fact, the Mulroney forces won every post on the Quebec executive. Mulroney, because of the Ritz Carlton meeting, felt he had created the perception of distancing himself from his supporters, who were preparing to overthrow Clark in Winnipeg. If I ever had any doubts about Mulroney's intentions, they were dissipated in late January 1983, as I boarded the Air Canada jet taking me from Dorval Airport in Montreal to Winnipeg. Mulroney and his wife, Mila, boarded the plane just before me, accompanied by a group of supporters. On the way out to Winnipeg, I sat in the front of the plane. At one point, Mulroney came forward and sat beside me, ostensibly just to have a general chat about the prospective proceedings at Winnipeg. He made absolutely no attempt to hide his contempt for Clark, and it was obvious what he had in mind. In Winnipeg, things were programmed to go wrong for Joe.

At the Winnipeg meeting, Clark got approximately the same support that he had received two years previously at the Ottawa convention. Incredible as it may seem, Clark felt this was not enough and called a leadership convention. This move merely added to my belief that, deep in his sub-conscious, Clark really didn't want to lead the party or to be prime minister. It seemed to me that the support he got was ample to allow him to carry on. By capitulating, he was opening the door to his eventual demise. In all fairness to Clark, there were other factors at work. Undoubtedly he did not want to carry on without the majority support within the caucus, which he knew he did not have. Mulroney supporters within the caucus had been active over the past several months.

Two members of Parliament, Elmer MacKay and Chris Speyer, had organized a letter-writing campaign within the caucus. Individual members who did not want to write directly to Clark, telling him to quit, gave sealed letters to MacKay and his group, letters indicating that they had withdrawn their support from the leader. These letters would be made public if and when a majority of the caucus had turned against the leader who would not quit if he should obtain an as yet undetermined percentage of the vote in Winnipeg. Friends of Clark, such as Harvie Andre of Calgary, told him that the caucus uprising was not significant, but this was incorrect.

Sometime before the Winnipeg meeting, the caucus had to elect a chairman. Bill McKnight was Clark's choice, and Ron Huntington was supported by the anti-Clark faction. Huntington won out. While the extra-parliamentary wing of the party would largely support Clark at Winnipeg, the caucus proved to be a major factor in his downfall. Clark's error, it could be argued, was in insisting he have 70% of the vote.

I happened to be outside the main convention hall on the first day of the proceedings when I witnessed Mulroney in an angry confrontation with the national press. One of his supporters, Jean-Yves Lortie, had showed up with two separate cheques amounting to $56,000, in order to register two hundred Quebec delegates *en bloc*. The practice was that delegates from across the country were meant to be registered individually before the convention got under way. Mulroney was virtually having a temper tantrum under the television lights, saying that the Quebec delegation was being "abused and humiliated by grossly overpaid party bureaucrats." All that was really happening was the Credentials Committee chief, MP Scott Fennell, held up their registration while their individual credentials were being verified. Mulroney termed this treatment "unforgivable, disgusting in the extreme."

Money and Politics

In the early fifties, a backroom Democratic "Pol" named Carmen de Sapio got out of a taxi in mid-town Manhattan. Unfortunately, he forgot his large black briefcase, leaving it in the cab as he debarked. When the driver opened the briefcase attempting to find the identity of his passenger, he found $350,000 in crisp, new U.S. bills. What de Sapio intended to do with these bills left little to the imagination.

In politics, money is the "sinews of war." Sometimes cheques are written but, more often than not hard cash, such as the money found in de Sapio's briefcase is the order of the day. Herein lies a problem that defies the very best efforts of lawmakers attempting to regulate expenditures and money-raising in the political arena. Here are a few examples. Before the 1958 elections, I arrived home at around midnight and found an envelope on my desk. It was from a fellow I knew who desperately wanted to be named a superior court judge. In the envelope was $5,000 in crisp fifty-dollar bills. I re-sealed the envelope and the next day put it into the hands of my official agent and so informed the donor who was, to say the least, not pleased. During the same election period, from time to time, people would leave a few large bills with me as we shook hands. They would look puzzled when I told them to give the bills to my official agent. Before the 1968 election, a corporate leader met me in the law offices of one of my organizers in Magog, Quebec. He handed me $1,000 in cash with the admonition "don't tell anybody." When I told him to give the money to my official agent, he was furious. There's the rub. No lawmaker or regulator can police or enforce the simple transition involving the handing of money from one person to another. To compound the felony, if the monies so issued are used to purchase goods or services for an election campaign, the cash is often passed "under the table" and no receipts are involved. So much for honest reporting procedures for election expenses after the completion of a campaign.

What about the matter of goods and services? In England, in the 1950s, when it was thought a future Labour government would nationalize the sugar industry, Tate and Lyle, the UK's biggest sugar producer, printed pro-Tory and anti-Labour slogans on sugar cube wrappers. In Canada, who costs the time spent by union officials working for the NDP while "on the job"?

Power Corporation placed its corporate jet at the disposal of Brian Mulroney when he sought the Tory leadership in 1976. Liberal leadership hopeful John Turner also used corporate jets for political purposes. Apart from the obvious potential for conflict of interest, we can be sure that the expenditures involved in their use were neither reported nor investigated. Before and after the Mulroney years, hard cash played a huge part in his rise and fall. After all, it was in the area of fundraising that he got his feet wet in the political arena. As I watched the delegates from Quebec duly registered in 1963, I asked myself, "Where did the money come from?" During the 1976 leadership race, as already noted, all candidates with the exception of Mulroney had agreed to divulge the source of funds raised. Michael Meighen, now a senator and a Mulroney supporter, protested. He said it was impossible to make public the names of donors. Once more, I asked myself, "What does Mulroney or his donors have to hide?"

Later in June of 1983, after the convention that named Mulroney leader, I sensed I had part of the answer. Michel Cogger had a farm outside the town of Brome Lake where I lived. On a hot June day in 1983, he hosted, at his farm, a huge reception for the new leader with a large tent and first-class food and drink. The party faithful came from far and wide. Once they gathered, a large helicopter was seen hovering over the Cogger farm. After landing, the leader was enthusiastically greeted with chants of "Brian! Brian!" Walter Wolf was at Mulroney's side. Wolf was the mysterious offshore businessman who had helped Mulroney dethrone Clark. As Wolf brushed by me, referring to Clark, he said, "We got the bastard." I had visions of Jean-Yves Lortie in Winnipeg. And so it goes.

What to do? My great friend Jacques Tétrault has been a hugely successful corporate lawyer practising in Montreal. He had the reputation of being able to draft the very best and relatively short corporate contracts. Once he said to me, "Heward, give me the best corporate contract and, unless there is honesty and goodwill, you can drive a truck through many of its clauses." When I was in business, most of my major deals were verbal, often based on goodwill and a handshake.

Almost to a day of the first anniversary of the November 27, 2000 election, House speaker Jean-Pierre Kingsley tabled his 172-page report on funding. He advocated that all leadership candidates and riding associations should be forced to report openly all monies received. He went on to report, "Currently, the money that politicians and parties are required to report is just a fraction of what pours into party coffers." When all is said and done, Government House leader Don Boudria gave little hope that Kingsley's key recommendations would ever find their way into legislation. As Major Bowes used to say when introducing his famous network radio show in the thirties, "Around and around the old wheel goes and where it stops nobody knows."

When I think of money and politics, I think of Tétrault's observations. Although goodwill and honesty make things go round in the real world, our goal should be to have enforceable laws and regulations. "Enforceable" is the elusive catch word.

The Sunday morning after Clark had made the dramatic announcement that he would call a leadership convention, I met briefly with him, and pledged my support. Quite frankly, I was faced with a dilemma. Much of the party was angry at Clark for losing power the way he had, and I must say I shared these sentiments.

Between mid-February and early March it became apparent that Mulroney was getting ready to declare his leadership bid. To his intimates and some key members of the press corps he let it be known what his intentions were. By this time, Mulroney had approximately a dozen full-time workers toiling in an office on de Lorimier Avenue in Montreal, and on March 9, 1983 a "Friends of Brian Mulroney Dinner" was held in the ballroom of Montreal's Queen Elizabeth Hotel. Keith Morgan, one of Mulroney's key supporters, had played a large role in organizing it. On March 21, the day after he had gone to Sept-Iles for a farewell meeting with the employees of Iron Ore Company of Canada, the company he headed for seven years, he officially announced his campaign for the party leadership. John Crosbie also announced his candidacy on the same day.

The leadership campaign was extremely controversial in the way it was waged. The delegate-selection meeting in Brome-Missisquoi was but one example of the tricks that were used. In Longueuil, a Clark partisan succeeded in having Mulroney's official representatives barred from the delegate-selection meeting.

In all my political experience, one particular riding meeting in 1983 was the saddest event for me. Delegates were to be chosen from my riding of Brome-Missisquoi to attend the PC leadership convention to be held in June in Ottawa. Clark and Mulroney were the principal leadership contenders. The local party executive, under the direction of its president, Louis Cournoyer, had held a number of preparatory meetings. Our association membership was approximately one thousand, and only card-carrying members in good standing could vote at the delegate-selection meeting. I had to explain this principle; the idea of membership cards had never been accepted by the local association, and none of its members possessed a card. The requirement for membership cards was handed down by the party's national executive, and I persuaded Cournoyer and the rest of the executive of the necessity to get out and sell membership cards to the association members on our lists—lists that had been built up over the previous twenty-five years. They did a reasonably good job and sold about four hundred cards. They made no attempt to influence individual party members in favour of one candidate or another. I was publicly supporting Clark, but my hope for the meeting was to see party workers sent to Ottawa who would weigh the candidates thoughtfully and vote for their considered choice as the best leader. The party executive knew that the Mulroney organization was active in the riding. They felt that selling four hundred membership cards to established party supporters would be enough to offset any practices that might undermine the democratic intent of the process.

Brian Mulroney had a lot of friends who had summer residences in the riding, but whose roots were mainly in Montreal or elsewhere. None of them had ever worked in the local association or in local elections.

Michel Cogger directed the campaign for Mulroney in Brome-Missisquoi with what seemed like limitless funds.

It was a cool day in the early spring of 1983 when I drove from Ottawa to Cowansville with Professor Luc Fortin of the University of Ottawa. The meeting was to be held at the local community centre. As Fortin and I drove into the parking area of the centre, my heart sank. Apart from the two hundred or so cars one expects to see at such events, there were also about twenty yellow school buses.

In the hall, I took a seat alongside Louis Cournoyer. Sitting quietly to my left were long-time members of the association. They had come from every corner of the riding, and I knew each one of them by name. Most of the thousand or so bussed-in participants were screaming adolescents, with the exception of the Mulroney operatives, who looked glamorous enough to have just left a nearby cocktail party. I had never before seen such richly dressed and haughty people at a political rally in that area. The great majority were the children of well-to-do Montrealers, mostly weekenders from the Brome Lake area. This operation probably constituted a first exposure to public affairs for most of them. The Mulroney slate of delegates was circulated. It took Chairman Cournoyer some time to establish order as the screaming young people continued to chant, "Brian! Brian! Brian!" In view of my long involvement in the riding and the party, Cournoyer asked me to address the meeting. I was loudly booed for several solid minutes, the first time I had ever experienced that reaction from people in my own party in all my political career. The booing reached a crescendo as I told the crowd that while it was no secret which leadership candidate I supported, I had in no way attempted to influence others in the association, and that included Cournoyer himself. The younger participants continued to boo and hiss. Perhaps because of their cynical introduction into the political process, they found it hard to believe that there were still people who care more about how the game is played than about winning. I noted that while Cournoyer had been the association's president for twenty-five years and had fought alongside me during ten federal elections, I had no idea how he would vote. Because of his service to the party, I hoped that those present would unanimously name him a delegate to the convention. I was dreaming. The boos increased. Cournoyer was not selected as a delegate, and the Mulroney slate was voted in.

In the parking lot, Mulroney's people shouted insults at me. The old-time members filed out of the hall in funeral fashion. Few of the Mulroney contingent at this meetings are members of the association today. Many of them threw away their membership cards in the parking lot after the vote. Cournoyer quit the association, as did many other members. Mulroney sent emissaries to appease him. The new leader even wished to present him with some sort of plaque in recognition of his past services when he next visited the riding. He had seriously underestimated the pride and self-esteem of people like Cournoyer. The honours were not accepted. The damage to the party's unity was not to be so easily repaired.

A man, who as a party president had helped me win seven elections under an enormous handicap in Quebec was denied a voice in selecting a new leader. One of Mulroney's stalwart supporters said to me recently over lunch in Montreal, "Heward, when will you get with it and realize how the game is played?" I thought to myself, did he not realize that short-term expediency often leads to long-term disaster.

Later in the day, after the delegate-selection meeting, I returned to my home. Journalists telephoned for interviews. One caller asked how I felt now that I was no longer the "boss" of the PC Association in Brome-Missisquoi. I told him I had never been the boss, but he didn't seem to understand.

The significance of this story lies not in the fate of one vote in one riding, but in the way people with influence and money can cut their own path to positions of political power. It is about the subverting of democracy. What happened in my riding happened in many ridings, with minor variants. We need to consider the process and regain our right of democratic choice. We need to regain our respect for our leaders by selecting leaders who have earned our respect.

In the Montreal riding of St-Jacques, twenty voters from a men's hostel were bussed to a meeting by Mulroney supporters. The men flashed copies of Old Brewery Mission identification cards to receive their ballots. Asked about the presence of the men from the hostel, a Mulroney organizer said, "They're very conscientious electors. I hope there'll be some beer for them later." Sure enough, when the ballots were counted and Mulroney's slate had won by twenty-seven votes, cases of beer were carted out from the hall's kitchen.

Mulroney supporters complained that attempts were made to mislead would-be voters in Verchères riding by giving them false information about the date of the meeting. Joe Clark's summary of the campaign might have been intended for his political tombstone. "Democracy is sometimes messy," he said to a reporter a few days before the convention.

About the end of May, in Edmonton an agent from Mulroney's campaign, along with the agents of four other candidates, began discussing a deal to beat Clark. At that time, the so-called anybody-but-Clark strategy was thrashed out. Mulroney had traveled almost 40,000 miles and had visited nearly all the federal ridings from coast to coast. Learning from his unsuccesful 1976 bid for power, he made a determined effort to play down any show of extravagance. By the time the convention opened in Ottawa on the weekend starting June 10, 1983, the die had pretty much been cast.

I sat with Joe Clark and his family and with other former leadership candidates from the party, including Bob Stanfield and Duff Roblin, and at the end of nine hours and four ballots in intense heat at the crowded Civic Centre, Mulroney drowned Clark by 1,584 votes to 1,325. At 9:20 p.m. on Saturday, June 11, 1983, Brian Mulroney was declared the victor.

In the convention hall, national television caught me in a very private moment, looking sad, with my head in my hands. It was partly fatigue and partly a deep sense of sympathy for Joe Clark and his family beside me in the box. It was also the realization that my high school dream and parliamentary career had come to an end with Mulroney as the new party leader—a leader who had never held elective office and about whom I had the most profound misgivings.

CHAPTER FIVE

Mulroney-Campbell-Charest, and Clark Recycled

At the conclusion of the June 1983 convention that named Brian Mulroney leader of the Progressive Conservative Party, I opted out of public life. I had no desire to serve in Parliament under him. He also had no desire to have me as a member of the Progressive Conservative caucus, let alone as a minister in his Government. Between 1983 and 2000, I was an observer of public affairs. I have never lost my interest or passion for political life at the federal level. Mulroney and I approached government affairs with diametrically opposite views. He organized from the top down. This resulted in a form of elitism that I found unacceptable—elitism that all parties up until that time, including the NDP, were guilty of. The convention that nominated Mulroney and the tactics used in pre-convention manoeuvring were a showcase of corruption where the grass roots were totally forgotten and ignored.

It seemed not long after Mulroney got his feet under his desk, Canadians read with great frequency that either a backbencher or a minister got caught with his or her hands in the cookie jar. Party supporters tell me the Liberals, today, are just as bad.

In 1987, Suzanne Blais-Grenier, the Tory environment minister, urged Mulroney to clean house. When he did nothing about her complaint, she blew the whistle by saying a kickback network existed. The Prime Minister turfed her out of caucus and into political oblivion.

Mulroney's pronouncements on patronage matters, "Ya dance with the lady that brought ya," while true in part, did not go over well with the public over the long term. The damage done was real. Eventually Canadians had enough of Mulroney's extravagant lifestyle. In a day when leadership style amounts to substance, Mulroney gradually but surely landed the PC Party in deep trouble with the electorate.

In Quebec after the spring of 1983, the hard day-to-day work of grass roots organization was ignored. Instead, Mulroney joined hands with his old Liberal friend, Robert Bourassa, to cobble together an informal electoral pact for the elections coming in 1984. He also reached out to the separatist elements in the province in order to get them on board. A case in point was his old college friend, Lucien Bouchard, who was eventually appointed ambassador to France. This was an understandable initiative on the part of Mulroney, as he was offering, at the time, a renewed federalism for Quebec that would allow them to join the "Canadian family with honour."

Before the election there were strong rumours that Mulroney would run in my old riding of Brome-Missisquoi where the results had been good in 1980. Perhaps because he was aware of my organizers' and my attitude towards him, he opted not to run in Brome-Missisquoi and chose instead to run in the riding of Manicouagan, which included his home town of Baie Comeau. Some weeks before the 1984 election, the phone rang in my Knowlton office. It was Gilles Mercure, my agent in the last three elections in which I ran. He said Mulroney wanted Gabby Bertrand to be the candidate in Brome-Missisquoi and wanted to announce her candidacy the next day. I liked her. She had been married to the late Jean-Jacques Bertrand, former Union Nationale premier of the province. He had been a member of the National Assembly from Missisquoi. Gabby was born into the Giroux family, a family of real "bleus." Her brother Fernand was one of my excellent organizers. Mercure, later to be named a superior court judge by Mulroney, was with Michel Cogger.

I said on the phone to Mercure, "But what about an open convention, duly called with advanced publicity, by the elected party executive?"

Mercure replied, "Heward, Michel Cogger informs me you are ready to waive the necessity for a nominating convention."

"That is not true," I asserted. "I never spoke with Cogger or said such a thing. All my successful elections, all of them," I told Mercure, "were preceded by an open convention where the delegates from each polling division confirmed my nomination—even if I was not opposed."

It was too late. The very next morning Mulroney announced Gabby's candidacy. Despite reservations regarding the process, I worked hard for her during the election, attending public meetings and visiting factory gates in the early hours of the morning to shake hands with workers.

By now, the stage was set for the election. Pierre Trudeau saw the writing on the wall and quit. It was said he jumped ship—after a long winter's walk during a snowstorm in 1984 outside Sussex Drive. The press reported he weighed the pros and cons of his future in politics. Give me a break; he knew he could not win another election.

Before he left office, Trudeau made a number of controversial patronage appointments. It seems his successor, John Turner, had little choice but to confirm these appointments, as he had undoubtedly guaranteed Trudeau that we would go along with the nominations. During the election campaign, Mulroney confronted Turner, the new prime minister, during a television debate, asking him why he did such a foolhardy thing.

"I had no choice," replied Turner. "Yes, you did," retorted Mulroney, dramatically jabbing an accusing finger at the forlorn Turner. It was a major triumph for Mulroney as a novice campaigner. Mulroney led the Progressive Conservatives to power on September 4, 1984, with a landslide 211 seats—the Liberals and NDP getting 40 and 30 seats, respectively. It was the beginning of an eight-year reign before the party plummeted to an abysmal two seats in the election of October 25, 1993.

Much went right for the Tory government, but much went wrong. On the plus side was the goods and services tax (GST) and the free trade agreement with the U.S. In previous elections, business leaders told me about their desire to have a GST-like tax initiative put into place. Mulroney would bring their wishes to realization. Because of bad advice from officials at "Finance," the GST got off to a bad start. Broad principles of the legislation were badly explained to the public. The Opposition went on the attack and Michael Wilson, the finance minister, was hurt and in trouble. Eventually, the GST gained public acceptance. The Grits said they would abolish it once in power but never did.

The election of November 21, 1988, was largely fought over free trade with the U.S. Business leaders such as David M. Culver, chairman and CEO of the Aluminium Company of Canada, came out on television in support of Mulroney's free trade initiative. Opposition leader John Turner lost a lot of support from the business community when he reversed his original position, panicked, and turned against the free trade initiative. Mulroney retained power on November 21, 1988, with 169 seats, to the Liberals' 83. Perhaps Turner remembered the political implications of Sir John A. Macdonald's national policy without realizing times had changed. The free trade pact between Canada and the U.S. was signed on January 2, 1988.

Mulroney dearly wanted to update constitutional provisions to bring Quebec back into the Canadian fold. The Meech Lake Accord followed by the Charlottetown Accord were his two kicks at the can and he failed badly. Questions of constitutional matters rarely electrify the Canadian electorate, unless politicians mess up with them. Meech Lake and Charlottetown were two cases in point.

It is hard to guess whether anything would have kept Lucien Bouchard, who had become minister of the environment, on the Government benches during the Meech crisis. My view is that he and Jean Charest got into a turf war. Charest's initiatives during the Meech Lake hearings in Parliament's Railway Committee room were disastrously flawed. They were rushed and superficial and in no way did Charest consult the grass roots. During Meech, when leaders ultimately huddled behind closed doors, the public felt left out. Mulroney's "rolling the dice" declaration gave little credence to this major matter. There is a perception that the provinces ultimately sounded the death knell for Meech, but they were aided and abetted by the incredibly inept handling of this initiative by Mulroney and his supporters.

The next move for constitutional reform came about with the Charlottetown proposals. Mulroney and his cohorts reminded me of a student ready to write a supplementary exam. The only trouble was he had not done his homework and was no more prepared for Charlottetown than he had been for Meech. The Prime Minister had transferred Joe Clark from external affairs into the inter-governmental affairs portfolio. He handed Joe a hot potato. Clark was totally over his head in the handling of the matter. At this time I was seeing a lot of Pierre Trudeau. During lunch one day we talked about the Charlottetown referendum. He reluctantly said he thought it would pass. I observed that we should never underestimate the intelligence of the electorate. Trudeau and I, albeit for different reasons, opposed Charlottetown. When he said Mulroney was merely a head waiter to the provinces, he meant it. We both felt that Charlottetown would so emasculate the federal authority, that nothing much would be left for Ottawa to do or initiate.

Pierre read to me, over the phone, the article he wrote for *Maclean's* magazine opposing Charlottetown and he quoted lines from a text for a speech he was about to give at a public forum sponsored by the magazine *Cité Libre* at a Chinese restaurant in Montreal. Both the *Maclean's* article and his restaurant speech received great publicity from coast to coast. At a subsequent meal, Pierre said he felt his thrusts would have little effect and wouldn't change much. Was this false modesty? I think not. Pierre almost always meant what he said. I disagreed with his observation and noted that while he had been out of public affairs for some years, his opinions had weight. The vote on the Charlottetown Accord was held on October 26, 1992—the rest is history. It went down to defeat.

Mulroney, with his initiatives on free trade and the GST, fulfilled the conservative side of the party's agenda. He should be congratulated for that. On the other hand, he left totally unfulfilled the progressive side of the party's agenda. In effect, no progressive social initiatives were advanced during his eight years in power. Mulroney was finally caught in a Catch 22 bind. People, both on the left and right of centre, thought he had done too little. In the context of Canadian politics, this spelled disaster.

Kim Campbell

The stage was set for yet another convention to name a new party leader. It was my hope that the party would adopt the "one member–one vote" method for leadership selection which I had recommended to the party in the mid-eighties. I was ready to support Kim Campbell and appealed to her office long before the convention date to have the "one member-one vote" rule invoked. It was too late and the old rules would be enforced, resulting in yet another of the traditional conventions.

The leadership convention was held in Ottawa and Campbell was named leader on June 25, 1993. I cannot say I knew her very well, but I admired her past performance as justice minister. She was obviously extremely intelligent and I could not hide my pride in the fact that my party gave Canada its first woman prime minister. I had met her from time to time, once with her mother at the cash line-up at a food store near my home in central Ottawa. She was extremely personable and pleasant. After her nomination, Campbell had the wind in her sails, as indicated by the polls. The polls held steady in her favour right up till the time she called an election on September 8, 1993, for October 25. The polls continued in her favour during the early days of the campaign but then the roof fell in on her and the party. All sorts of Monday morning quarterbacks laid the blame at her feet for a bad election performance. She did her best but was in an impossible situation. I felt, in fact, she was a sacrificial lamb paying dearly for the sins of the Mulroney years. Canadians were furious at Mulroney—and Campbell, and her candidates were to pay the price at the polls. On election day, Jean Chrétien was elected and the only two members of our party members to survive the Liberal avalanche were Jean Charest from Sherbrooke and Elsie Wayne from St. John. The great party of Macdonald and Cartier had been totally humiliated. When things start looking bad for individual members of parliament and party leaders, they sense which way the wind is blowing. Rather than stay and fight, they leave. Before the election of Kim Campbell as leader, Mulroney jumped ship, followed by Joe Clark who saw the writing on the wall in his old riding of Rocky Mountain, Alberta. The captain and his senior lieutenant bailed out while Campbell and the Tory ship sank to the bottom of the electoral ocean. There were only two survivors and the rest drowned in a sea of Liberals.

Politics as an Honourable Profession

The public reacts seriously against the idea of people enriching themselves directly or indirectly by entering public life. Teachers, religious leaders, social and community workers, and others go into their professions with little or no idea of eventually becoming rich. Of course, they should and must be paid enough to meet their bills but they get their main satisfaction from a job well done in an area of concern that challenges and motivates them. Great wealth, unless inherited, is not in the cards for them. The same should hold true for public life. Mulroney's rich lifestyle turned off the voters. There was public revulsion at the fact that Progressive Conservative party officials handed over to Claude Wagner a $300,000 trust fund. At present, the Progressive Conservative party is millions of dollars in debt and senior party officials have been obliged to raid the party's trust fund in order to keep the party afloat. Joe Clark is receiving an MP's salary and I assume will have a prime minister's pension. When he assumed the leadership of the party in 1998, he negotiated an annual salary from the party of well over $100,000 per annum and as I write, he is still being remunerated by the party. This is simply not right. Hundreds of MPs, past and present, live very frugally in small apartments in Ottawa. Clark should have set an example.

"Good luck on the road to Parliamentar Hill" were the first words of encouragement I received in my high school graduation magazine in the spring of 1946. To be a member of Parliament, representing thousands of people in the highest court of the land, was my boyhood dream. At first I wanted to be a doctor, and, a little later, I yearned to be a medical missionary, but a high school visit to Ottawa gave me a new resolve. My family and friends never held politicians in high esteem so I received little outside encouragement, except for the odd reference to the lofty ideals of the public service, which did not necessarily include the pursuit of elective office.

In 1958, at the age of twenty-nine, I was sworn into the House of Commons as the new member for Brome-Missisquoi. A that time, the riding was approximately 70% French-speaking. Since my mother tongue was English, I considered it a great honour and responsibility to represent such an electorate. Between 1957 and 1980, I stood as a candidate in ten federal elections, and most of my years in the House were spent on the Opposition benches. There were frustrations, but my advice to anyone contemplating public service in the House of Commons is: "Give it a try." Young people ask me when is the right time for them to stand. The truth is that there never really is a right time. Every individual intuitively knows when they should take the plunge. It is a personal decision.

Service in the House is a rewarding experience, with endless satisfactions. It requires sacrifices, but so does all worthwhile work. The hours are long and the telephone problems sometimes seem insoluble, but anybody holding a seat in the Commons who is willing to work hard is given unbounded scope to get things done. With a little creative imagination, the life of a parliamentarian becomes fascinating and, in John Buchan's words, an "honourable adventure."

Helping constituents solve problems with their pensions, their family allowances, and employment insurance cheques, working to bring a new industry into the riding, speaking out on national issues in caucus and in the House were but a few factors that made the job fulfilling for me.

Our next leader and future prime minister must set an example and encourage party members in each riding to nominate candidates to carry the party banner to victory—candidates who will live up to the ideals described above.

When my days in public service were over in 1980, I left my constituency association with $25,000 in the constituency account, one thousand listed PC members in the riding, and a duly elected party executive. Twenty years later, before the elections of November 27, 2000, when I started to work once more in the riding, there was no money in the account, no riding executive, and no listed members. So much for the elitist years of Stanfield, Mulroney, and Clark. Recently in Brome-Missisquoi, we had a meeting and elected a party executive and have set an objective of selling membership cards to one thousand people before May 15, 2002. This objective will be met.

Jean Charest

Soon after the elections, Campbell gave up the leadership of the party and retired from active politics. Jean Charest, in effect, became the ex-officio leader of the party.

In terms of getting the Speaker's eye in the Commons, Charest was in an impossible situation. Only on rare occasions was he recognized during question period as his party's profile virtually drifted out of sight. He soldiered on as best he could. His moment of glory came in the referendum called by Quebec Premier Jacques Parizeau for October 30, 1995. Jean Charest did a magnificent job touring the province on behalf of the "NO" forces. I met him at the huge rally in Montreal a number of days before the vote. He spoke with force and conviction. I also met with Pierre Trudeau a few days after the rally. He had severe reservations about how Chrétien was leading the "NO" forces. In fact, Chrétien's leadership in this instance was seriously flawed. I told Trudeau the vote was too close to call. After the results of the referendum were in, it is more than arguable that Charest had saved the day for the "NOs."

At the next federal election, June 2, 1997, Jean Charest led his forces back to party status with twenty members in the House. Things were looking much better and the party's profile benefited as its members were now more frequently recognized during question period.

What happened next was for me, unspeakable. In Quebec, Daniel Johnson resigned as leader of the Liberal Opposition in the National Assembly. I felt badly for Johnson. I have much respect for him, as I had for his father and brother. Surely, I thought, the Liberals would find a replacement for Johnson from within their own provincial ranks. Pressure built up, especially in English Canada, for Jean Charest to abandon his Ottawa forces and take up the leadership of the Quebec Liberals. How can he? I mused. He's a blue Tory. This didn't seem to matter anymore. Tory fundraisers, most of whom subsequently jumped ship and opted for the Alliance, told Charest that unless he took up the Quebec challenge, the funding tap would be turned off for his federal party. To this day, I don't believe Charest ever wanted to be Liberal leader in Quebec. He was blackmailed. Hysteria prevailed in English Canada. He was told it was his duty to go and save Canada. What nonsense, I thought. For me, there never was, isn't now, and never will be, an indispensable saviour for Canada. Just as my party was getting back on its feet in Ottawa, the captain abandoned ship—a ship that, once more, would become rudderless.

Much to my chagrin, Charest jumped into Quebec politics and was named the Liberal leader. It seems to me that, to date, his heart has not been in the job and his performance has been totally lacklustre. There are serious doubts whether or not he can compete with Premier Bernard Landry and his PQ forces at the next provincial election. Charest's father, Red, was always an old Union Nationale *bleu* going back to the time of Duplessis.

Charest's conversion from Tory blue to Liberal red did my party infinite harm in of Quebec. At the time of his conversion, the question of national unity had already been seriously politicized in Quebec. The party had opted out of serious grass roots organization in the province, had become marginalized, and was no longer a player in the National Unity debate. In effect, the Liberals were for Canada and the PQ for Quebec separation. This oversimplification of the question spelled disaster for the Progressive Conservative Party in Quebec, especially among English-speaking electors. Many of my old organizers gave up the ship in order to vote Liberal and save Canada. During the campaign for the November 2000 federal election, Quebec Tory candidates were insulted because they were told they were splitting the federal vote and encouraging separation. By then, the Liberal government was well on its way to ruining what was, heretofore, the best public health scheme in the world. Even this major question was not an election issue as the Liberal scare tactics on unity held Quebec federalists in a straitjacket of fear. In Quebec, the election was the Liberals for Canada versus the Bloc Québécois for Quebec and separation. All other parties were out of the race. Charest's conversion or defection to the Liberal cause did much to aid and abet the disastrous effects on my, and his, old party, especially in Quebec.

Chrétien was even more imaginative in getting rid of Charest as the leader of the PC forces in the Commons. On three occasions, Chrétien invited Charest to his office telling him each time that if he didn't go to Quebec, he would be responsible for Quebec's separation if in fact this came about. Charest took the bait hook, line and sinker, and Chrétien, like Trudeau in 1976 with Wagner and Horner, got rid of a potentially significant opposition force in the Commons.

Charest was forced to work for the federal Liberals in the elections of November 2000. Chrétien used national unity as a weapon. Quebec electors were told that to save Canada they had to vote Liberal. The blame for this does not fall completely on the shoulders of Chrétien and the Liberal party. Stanfield, Mulroney, Clark, and the militants of the PC party, including myself, must share the blame.

To add insult to injury, when Charest left Ottawa for Quebec, he let it be known that he would never forget his blue friends in Ottawa and that, in effect, he would be neutral in relation to federal politics. What palpable nonsense. The hypocrisy of Charest's quasi-guarantee was there for all to see when the November 2000 federal elections got underway. In my riding of Brome-Missisquoi, Denis Paradis was, and still is, the federal Liberal member. His brother, Pierre, is and was the provincial member from the same riding. As the election got underway, a huge fundraising cocktail party was organized for Pierre, the provincial member. Charest was to be the guest speaker. I informed him by fax that if he turned up, I would consider his presence at the event a partisan act. He immediately announced that it was too late for him to cancel. He eventually turned up. So much for "neutrality." Charest knew only too well that when push comes to shove, Quebec provincial Liberals join hands with their Grit counterparts in Ottawa to fight federal elections.

The Recycling of Joe Clark

Many judgements we make in the political sphere are based on intuition. When Diefenbaker lost the 1963 general elections after letting his minority government fall, I knew he would never be prime minister again. The same holds true for Joe Clark. He let his minority government fall, called an election and lost it. While the party he leads could win the next election, the electorate does not find much to admire about Clark and does not see him as our next Prime Minister. As I write, I have no idea what Clark's intentions are. Diefenbaker's ultimate exit after his defeat took four years of infighting which inflicted serious wounds on the party. I hope Clark will not repeat the Diefenbaker performance. Like a father who lets this teenage son borrow the family car, the Canadian people gave power to Clark. After the teenage son crashed at high speed and totalled the family car, his father took back the keys, never to lend the car to his boy again. The same holds true for Clark. He was given power and, like Diefenbaker, he frittered it away. The public won't give Clark the keys to 24 Sussex Drive a second time.

With the absence of Charest in Ottawa there was a leadership vacuum in the party. The leadership selection process that elected Clark on October 24, 1998 was based on the "one member-one vote" method that the commission I headed in 1986 had recommend to the party. Votes were phoned in, sent in by mail, or faxed in. Clark won on the second ballot. Originally, there were approximately 40,000 eligible voters. I was disappointed with these numbers as, subsequently, the Alliance would sign up approximately 200,000 votes for the election of Stockwell Day as their leader.

For the next two years, Clark adamantly refused to seek a seat in the Commons. This refusal was based on the pretext that his main task would be to rebuild the party before the next elections were called. I have no idea what he did in this interim period but the facts are that when the writ went out calling the election for November 27, 2000, the party was woefully unprepared. It was millions of dollars in debt, only a handful of riding executives were duly elected by their constituency membership, and, unbelievably, very few party candidates had actually been nominated by the time Chrétien went to see the Governor General. In Quebec and Saskatchewan, for example, virtually no candidates had been nominated by the end of October 2000. While Clark kept insisting that the party would run candidates in every riding from coast to coast, he did virtually nothing to fulfill this guarantee. When he did, it was far too late.

On election day the Progressive Conservative Party was reduced to twelve members. Four of our sitting members from Quebec had crossed the floor to sit with the Liberals and were re-elected. I believe he could have kept the four Quebec members who jumped ship on board if he had reached out to them. Unbelievably, he did not.

Soon after the November election, the myth-makers and spin doctors got down to serious work. We were told, "the party had been saved." How going from 20 seats to 12 seats constitutes "being saved" baffles me. Once again, the party hierarchy relapsed into a state of denial. After the elections, we barely retained party status in the Commons. At the risk of seeming overcritical, let me state the following. Admittedly, the Alliance are the official Opposition in name and theory. Yet they abandoned their constitutional role and were imploding with internal strife over Day's leadership. Major issues such as health care are not being debated in the House. In a sense, Clark has co-opted the role as leader of the Opposition. This is to his credit but Shawinigate and the RCMP violence at the APEX Conference do not constitute the stuff that overthrows governments. As Clark attacked day after day on Shawinigate, I agreed that, at the least, Chrétien might have committed some indiscretion. On the other hand, at the heart of the matter was and is my sense that Canadians felt, and still feel, that Chrétien is a fundamentally honest man. The Liberals have become arrogant and assume they will be automatically re-elected automatically. This does not have to be the case, but the opposition must choose the right issues. The question of health care alone could and should defeat the government the next time out. Five years ago, we had the best health care system in the world. Now, it is ranked thirty-ninth. Paul Martin, without consultation, cut transfer payments to the provinces. He not only did not consult the provinces, he did not consult his own health minister in order to put together an action plan to save Medicare after the cuts. Reports today demonstrate that Canadians feel there is no federal leadership when it comes to preserving and upgrading our health care system. This is the sort of issue that defeats governments. It is my hope, as I write, that Joe Clark can seize this issue. The Liberal Government should not be let off the hook.

In the meantime, Clark must at least demonstrate a willingness for the party to initiate a membership drive with an objective of 350,000 new members. Presently the party has approximately 15,000 members signed up. Once we have reached the 300,000 members goal, a renewed leadership vote should be held. If Clark decides to run and wins, his credibility will be greatly enhanced and he could be prime minister again. If another candidate wins, he or she should enter Sussex Drive after the next election.

Riding executives would be voted in by party members in each constituency. Excellent candidates should be nominated in each riding by well-publicized and democratic local conventions at least one year before the next vote. Our army of 350,000 foot-soldiers would mean ten party members in each polling division engaging in guerilla warfare from coast to coast. If we do these things, victory will be ours next time out. If we do not, our party will disappear as a force on the national scene and one-party Liberal rule will continue. Clark has had over three years to get all these things done and has failed.

CHAPTER SIX

A Brief History of French Canada

In our attempt to alleviate Western and Quebec alienation and to seek constitutional renewal, we shall have to understand some of the history of these two regions. We do not know our strength if we do not know our history. In my case, I was taught a lot about European and American history in school and university. Canadian history was badly taught—if taught at all. I assume the same is true in our schools and universities today. The sense of our nation's past is largely non-existent. It is with this in mind that I include in this book separate histories of Quebec and the West. It is my hope that my efforts will promote understanding and unity and render the task easier for those working on constitutional reform initiatives that must come sooner rather than later.

Soon after I arrived in Ottawa in the spring of 1958, I remember observing circumstances which didn't seem significant at the time, but surely were, in many ways, harbingers of things to come. Even during those early years, Diefenbaker was adamant in expressing his views about "One Canada." In our general caucus, he forbade the formation of provincial caucuses among party members. Bill Hamilton, the postmaster general and member from Notre Dame de Grace in Quebec, attempted to organize regular meetings of the eight anglophone members recently elected from Quebec. I thought it was a bad idea and refused to attend. Hamilton's initiative came to an abrupt end, largely because of Dief's admonitions.

This state of affairs did not inhibit certain caucus members. I could not help but notice that our francophone members sat *en bloc* at one end of the railway committee room during our regular weekly meetings and our western members did the same. Both groups, for different and obvious reasons, had historical grievances against Ottawa. Sir John A. Macdonald's trade and tariff policies together with the Crow's Nest freight rate policy constituted significant factors relating to western alienation. Since the western provinces joined Confederation after 1867, I felt that central Canada's insensitivity to their aspirations meant that they were often treated like new boys and second-class citizens in the Canadian family. Trudeau's energy policy was yet to come. Most of our Quebec members came from the nationalist *bleu* element in Duplessis' Union Nationale party. They shared Duplessis' grievances about the Liberals' centralization practices which made them, like their western *confrères*, unhappy members in the Canadian family. Little did I foresee, at the time, that I was witnessing the seeds of discontent that would be exacerbated over the ensuing forty years and resulting in the birth of two protest parties: the Alliance in the west and the Bloc in Quebec.

When I witnessed western and Quebec members sitting separately in our caucus, I could not help but feel that the leader and prime minister who could bring these forces of alienation together and channel their aspirations into the flow of a united Canada, would be rendering to Canada and its people a service of invaluable richness. Is it too late to accomplish and achieve this goal of unity today? I think not, but time is not on our side. To achieve such an end will take patience, creativity, imagination, good will, and a spirit of give-and-take making for productive compromise. Above all, it will take faith and genius. I live in hope. My Quebec separatist friends call me a dreamer. Yes, my dreams are big, but I don't intend to let them turn into nightmares. After all, and it has been said before, "politics is the art of the possible." I believe fundamental constitutional renewal is not only possible, it is essential for Canada. I agree with the observation of one of Quebec's leading nationalists, Dr. Philippe Hamel, who said, "Conquer us with good will, my English friends; you will be astonished at the easy victory that awaits you."

Quebec is unique among provinces in that it defines itself not in terms of its present, or even its future, but rather in terms of its history. To this day, no discussion of Quebec's place within Canada is complete without the necessary reference to the past. This became particularly evident during the proceedings of the Bélanger-Campeau Commission which was created by the Quebec government to consider Quebec's constitutional future. Virtually no day of the proceedings went by without the mandatory reference to the Durham Report or the consequences of the Battle of the Plains of Abraham. Even the Mouvement des Caisses Populaires Desjardins, one of Quebec's largest financial institutions, commissioned, and later presented to the Bélanger-Campeau Commission, a survey which began with a one-paragraph statement on the conquest of Quebec by the English. It is against such a historical backdrop that the future of Quebec within Canada will be played out. However, if Quebecers can be said to live their future against the backdrop of their past, English-speaking Canadians can be accused of ignoring theirs. For many English-Canadians, history began in Canada in 1759, the year of the Battle of the Plains of Abraham. The contributions made by the French before this date are often ignored and downplayed, let alone the accomplishments of the Native people who were here before the Europeans.

In the late 1950s francophone friends in Quebec invariably complained that Quebec anglophones were often more English that the English in the UK. They wondered how we could build a distinct Canadian nation as long as Quebec anglos persisted in this attitude.

Among those who voiced this complaint to me was my dear friend, the late Philippe Gélinas. Philippe was a courtly gentleman. He had braces on his legs and walked with a cane, having contracted polio as a youth on a scouting trip to Quebec's Gaspé Peninsula. I had met him as a law student at McGill during model parliament when he participated for the University of Montreal. He campaigned for me as a speaker in my early election of 1957 and 1958.

One morning, in my home town of Knowlton, I gave Philippe a wake-up call as we were scheduled to speak after the mass in a parish some forty miles away. Before leaving Knowlton I said, "Philippe, I have something to show you." Major General Basil Price was a nearby neighbour. He surely was more English than the English and a rabid monarchist to boot. After leaving the army, Price became head of the family business, Elmhurst Dairy, in Montreal West. Upon his retirement, his colleagues at the dairy presented him with a flag pole and a Union Jack. Each morning at Knowlton, before his breakfast, Price, with the Union Jack under his arm, would approach the flag pole which stood in front of his house. Once the flag was slowly raised to the top of the pole, the General snapped to a smart salute.

So, on the Sunday morning before our meeting, I took a chance. With Philippe in my car, I took a small detour and drove to the front of Price's house. Luck was on my side. Price emerged from his front door with the Union Jack dutifully tucked under his arm and he performed his usual flag pole routine with sombre precision. Gélinas was speechless.

History as a Force for Nationalism

History has been one the prime movers behind Quebec's nationalist movement. From the beginning the study of history in Quebec has been one which strived to explain the national character of Quebec and its survival in the face of the British Regime. The study of history in Quebec has tended to be more than just an accounting of the early years of the British Regime. Rather, historians like François-Xavier Garneau (1809-1866) used history to glorify the French-Canadian people and provided them with nationalistic ideas. For Garneau, history was "the power source of a national identity." His was an activist history.

At about the same time that Garneau's history of French Canada was being published in the mid-nineteenth century, John McMullen (1820-1907) was working on the first history from the English-Canadian perspective. McMullen's *The History of Canada from its First Discovery to the Present Time* was the first history of the country written by an inhabitant. Unlike Garneau, who saw his work as a challenge to Durham's Report, McMullen saw French Canadians as an impediment to the creation of a national Canadian identity. While French-Canada's elites perceived Lord Durham's Report as advocating cultural genocide, a still common interpretation among many Quebec intellectuals, McMullen saw it in the context of a positive contribution to the evolution of Canadian nationhood.

Early histories of Canada written from the English perspective also clashed with their French-Canadian counterparts in the way in which they defined Canadian nationhood and its relationship with the British Empire. While French-Canadian historians wrote of a "French-Canadian" nation with little link to France, English-Canadian histories were replete with statements on the virtues of British customs and institutions. In this context Quebec was seen as an encumbrance to these British traditions and connections being established in Canada. Furthermore, while many English-Canadian histories of the time were vehement in the way they chastised Quebec for blocking the development of the pan-Canadian nation, they often sounded like pro-British tracts in which Ontario was characterized as the guardian of British virtue and where preservation of the British link was paramount. Thus, while condemning their French-Canadian counterparts for having developed a national identity, English-Canadians were unwilling to define their own Canadian identity in terms other than British. This is one of the interesting paradoxes in which are rooted the sometimes widely divergent ways Quebecers and English-speaking Canadians see their country. This paradox persists and is one of the striking elements which differentiates the works of English Canadian and Quebec historians, beginning with Garneau and up to the present.

After Garneau came a number of French-Canadian historians. None, has been as influential as the controversial Father Lionel Groulx. Groulx's history freely blended the ideals of nationalism with a fervent Roman Catholicism. Writing under his own name and a pseudonym, Groulx argued for *la revanche des berceaux*, the revenge of the cradle, whereby through their high birthrate the French-Canadian people would eventually outnumber English-speakers in the other provinces.

Years later Groulx's influence can still be seen in the work of the historians such as Guy Frégault, Michel Brunet, and Maurice Séguin. The works of these historians shaped, to a great degree, the ideology and thinking of the independence movement. Guy Frégault's work, for example, reinforced the "national" thesis of Québécois sovereignists by arguing that the inhabitants of New France form a nation, different from the inhabitants of eighteenth century France. Others, such as Michel Brunet, returned to the "conquest" of French Canada and found in it the genesis of Quebec's struggle for independence. It is in this history that the "French Canadian" became the Québécois. These countless works have solidified in the minds of the masses the notion of national belonging for which defining oneself as different from other Canadians is essential. The Québécois became a people with nearly two hundred years of history behind them before being conquered by the British.

In 1834 Louis-Joseph Papineau published a document which set out the grievances of the Canadiens against the colonial government. His *Ninety-Two Resolutions* was despatched to London with a letter stating Papineau's intent to let the colony stagnate unless Britain acted upon the grievances. The response of the British government came four years later in the form of the *Ten Resolutions*, a document which authorized the Governor General to administer the province without the consent of the Assembly.

As a consequence of reduced trade with the United States the economy of Lower Canada did slow down. Stung by British intransigence and hurt by the recession, throngs of French Canadians, rich and poor, flocked to hear Papineau speak. Ignoring Papineau's pleas for restraint a number of men prepared to take up arms. It was after a speech by Papineau in St-Denis on November 22, 1837, that the first uprising against the British took place. Despite an early victory against a much larger and better-equipped British force, the Patriotes, as they were called, had little chance of achieving victory. Papineau, who had opposed the recourse to arms, fled to Vermont while his allies such as Louis-Hippolyte Lafontaine, hurried to Quebec City to arrange a peaceful settlement.

The aftermath of the rebellion was a period of political repression of the French-Canadians which culminated with the infamous Durham Report. The Durham Report advocated the forced assimilation of the French-Canadians through anglicization and the massive immigration of English-speakers to the province. While Durham's recommendations regarding assimilation never became the official policy of the British authorities, the report left the Canadiens unsure of their future under

British rule. This perception of insecurity has persisted to this day. Since 1838 the Canadiens were always suspected the intentions of the British, and assimilation by the English was forever a possibility which had to be averted at all cost. It is in these years that the nationalism of Garneau, Groulx, and all who followed in their footsteps found its genesis.

Lord Durham had little positive to say about the Canadiens, referring to them as people without literature, culture, and history and therefore without a future. In addition, Durham was very much influenced by the Montreal merchant class who argued that Canada was an economic unit and that the division between Upper and Lower Canada was having serious ill effects. The assimilation of the French Canadians, the recommendation most people associate with Durham, was incidental to the economic motives.

The Act of Union of 1840 did, in some ways, institute some of Durham's recommendations regarding the administration of the colony. Upper and Lower Canada were to be united into a single province of Canada with Canada West (Ontario) receiving a disproportionate share of political power compared to Canada East (Quebec). With a smaller population Canada West was granted more seats than Canada East in the legislative assembly. No majority of Patriotes could ever again disrupt or interfere with government operations.

The Act also contained a provision that would see the debts of both provinces merged into one single debt, a measure that benefited Canada West, with its very large debt, at the expense of the more fiscally responsible Canada East. While the Act of Union officially made English the only language of government of the new province, in reality this proved impractical and French continued to be used as it had in the past.

This is not to say that the French-speaking population was content with the situation. In fact the Act of Union encouraged the emigration of French Canadians from the Province of Canada because of their language. Fearing the prospect of forced assimilation, nearly 40,000 French Canadians left for the United States during the depressions of 1840 and 1850. It is around this period that a number of the Canadien elite began to see Confederation as the one political option which offered francophones the possibility of regaining some of the political power which they had lost to the English in general and to Canada West in particular.

When Confederation was first proposed by some English-Canadian politicians, the French-Canadian political elites were at first divided. Despite strong opposition from the nascent nationalist leadership in the province, much of the French-Canadian leadership eventually rallied behind George-Étienne Cartier and the federal solution because it offered Quebec control over language, religion, and the Civil Law. Cartier, supported by the unusual coalition of English Montreal merchants and the French-Canadian clergy, succeeded in achieving a federal solution for Quebec and convincing his fellow Quebecers to support the deal. On July 1, 1867, Quebec signed the British North America Act.

Quebec after Confederation

The history of Quebec in the years immediately following Confederation is one of a largely rural province struggling with the transformation to an industrial society, a change which challenged all of Canada, but which struck at the heart of the largely parochial organisation of Quebec society. During this period Quebec's industry was largely owned by Montreal's anglophone business class, while French educational and other institutions were controlled by the Catholic clergy. Its political system and institutions reflected the divisions which existed between the English Protestant and the French Catholic. Contributing to this backwardness was the federal government's preoccupation with the industrial development of Ontario. While the federal government provided Quebec with over 50% of its provincial budget, it neglected to concern itself with any other aspect of Quebec's industrialization. Quebec's government, short on cash and fraught with divisions, basically left the Church in charge of the social organisation of the province, thereby giving it a position unequalled in other provinces. The Church was preoccupied with its status and uninterested in promoting the modern era. This situation was to change progressively, although it is only well into the 1960s that Quebec's clergy can be said to have been removed from their position of influence in

Quebec society.

Paradoxically, one of the events which had the most lasting impact on the attitudes of French-Canadians with regards to Canada did not occur in Quebec. The Métis rebellion and the subsequent hanging of Louis Riel sounded the death knell of the provincial Conservatives in Quebec and reconfirmed, in the minds of French Canadians, that they were not welcome west of the Ottawa River. This theme would resurface after the Manitoba Schools decision, in which the use of French was disallowed, and still animates the discourse of many Québécois nationalist leaders to this day.

While the Canadiens were shocked at the violence of the rebellion in Manitoba the reaction of the Ontario Orangemen who demanded vengeance for the murder of Tom Scott, caused the Canadiens' leaders to close ranks behind Riel. After all, he and his people were mostly French-speaking and Riel himself had been educated in Montreal. While many Canadiens had not joined the drive to settle the western provinces, the Métis had become Canadiens by proxy.

Riel was portrayed by the Orangemen as a cruel and calculating rebel, but in Quebec he was perceived as a pathetic victim of his own dementia. Prime Minister Macdonald was swayed by the reaction of English Canada, and with the tacit approval of his three ministers from Quebec, Riel was hanged on November 16, 1885. Macdonald hoped that the political furor which divided English and French would die down, and it did, but the attitudinal differences persisted. As a prominent Quebec Conservative said at the time, "At the moment when the corpse of Riel falls through the trap and twists in the convulsions of agony, at that moment an abyss will be dug that will separate Quebec from English Canada."

The Quebec *Rouges*, the provincial Liberals, had sided with Riel from the beginning of his trial and had contributed to his defence team. For Honoré Mercier, the Liberal leader, the treatment of Riel by the federal government took on partisan aspects. The Conservatives and English-Protestant Canada had joined forces in the hanging of Riel. The trial itself revealed a strong anti-French undercurrent in English Canada and Liberal politicians in Quebec attempted to capitalize on this.

On November 22, 1885, a mass rally in Montreal was organized to protest Riel's hanging. Among the speakers who addressed the thousands of people who crowded into Montreal's historic civic square, Champs-de-Mars, were Honoré Mercier and Wilfrid Laurier. Both spoke of the tragedy of the Riel saga and equated his hanging with hanging French Canada.

Quebec was changed by the Riel Affair. In Riel, Quebec saw someone who tried to get more out of Canada and was hanged for his efforts. If Quebec, which also hoped to get more out of Confederation, was to escape the same fate it would have to band together. Quebec from now on would be *Rouges* (Liberal) rather than the *Bleus* (Conservative).

While Confederation had been profitable to French-Canadian lawyers, politicians, clergy, and a few business people, the levers of economic power remained in the hands of English-Protestant Montrealers. Slums and low wages for the French Canadians were compared to the mansions of English Montreal. The feeling of being exploited by Confederation simmered in the minds of many Canadiens and and suddenly came to the fore in the aftermath of the Riel affair. Mercier seized on these feelings of isolation and impotence to try and achieve political power. In the provincial elections of 1886, Mercier won a crushing majority, a result widely interpreted as a protest vote against the Conservatives in Ottawa.

It is during this period that some alternative views of Quebec's place in Confederation began to emerge. Among these was the notion that Confederation was a compact between two founding nations, English Canada and French Canada. According to this view it was the provinces and not Ottawa which were the sovereign powers in Confederation. Ottawa had therefore usurped its power and had stolen from Quebec the benefits of Confederation.

Many French Canadians opted to leave the province for the United States during this period. While the cause of this emigration, as with the emigration of the 1840s, was the economic crisis, it is interesting to note that only a few thousand French-Canadians chose to settle in the western provinces. Meanwhile half a million left for the U.S., a country where their language and culture were much more at risk than in Canada. Again, as with the Durham Report, the treatment of Riel reinforced the perception that French-Canadians were not in fact equal to other Canadians and that they were expected to remain locked within the geographical confines of Quebec.

Boosted by American demand for its natural resources, the economy of the province grew nearly 80% after 1910. Although agriculture still accounted for most of its economic output, the manufacturing sector was continuing to grow, mostly in the Montreal area. By the outbreak of World War I the manufacturing sector accounted for over one-third of the Quebec's gross domestic product.

The government of the province was firmly in the hands of the Liberal Party after Riel, and the party's domination of federal politics in Quebec was further entrenched as a consequence of the imposition of conscription in 1918. As Macdonald had done with Riel, Borden significantly misread public opinion in Quebec and this error in political judgement further widened the divide separating Quebec from English Canada. Prime Minister Borden's attempt to capitalize on the anti-conscription feeling in the province of Quebec divided the country to an unprecedented extent.

In the early months of World War I, while public opinion in both French and English Canada favoured Canada's war effort as a patriotic duty to Britain, French Canada's support was more circumspect. While some demonstrations took place in Montreal in support of the war effort, few Canadiens supported conscription as a means of filling the ranks of Canada's expeditionary force. French Canadians were eager to contribute to the war effort so long as this was a voluntary contribution. However, domestic political issues would soon turn French Canadians against the war and the government of the day, this leading to one of Canada's most trying national unity crises.

Following the declaration of war in 1914, Prime Minister Borden had promised that Canada's army would be made up of volunteers. However, by 1916 recruitment for the war in Europe began to wane and the losses from the trench war were mounting. For Canadian commanders and their British supervisors, getting adequate reinforcements to the front became a major preoccupation.

The issue of conscription resurfaced following Prime Minister Borden's return from the Imperial War Conference of May 1917. For Borden the war offered Canada the opportunity to become a truly independent nation from Great Britain, while at the same time strengthening the ties between the former colony and the Mother Country. Consequently, Borden did not see any other options. If Canada was to grow as a nation, and at the same time keep the faith with England, it would be necessary to send its sons to war.

Unfortunately for Borden the question of Ontario's French-language schools soon became the issue in the hearts and minds of Quebec's French Canadians. The law, Rule 17, proposed to abolish all French-language schooling in Ontario. The issue of conscription became the vehicle by which Quebec's political and social elites articulated their dissatisfaction with the treatment of French Canadians in Ontario. Rule 17 also sent conflicting messages to French Canadians for they were asked to die in defence of freedom and liberty in Europe while the rights of their cousins were curtailed in the neighbouring province. From this point onwards the elite in French Canada began to alter its position on the war. The first line of defence for French Canada wasn't in Flanders but in Ottawa. Even the creation in 1914 of a French Canadian Regiment, the Royal Twenty-Second or "Vandoos," as they were known in English Canada, did nothing to encourage French Canadians to sign up for the war.

French Canada's support for the war evaporated at the same time as Canada's war effort began to falter due to dropping enlistment. Borden's people returned from the Imperial War Conference convinced conscription was necessary and he announced his decision to Parliament on May 18, 1917. Borden at first offered to form a political coalition with Wilfrid Laurier's Liberals. Laurier's own choices were limited, however.

Quebec, he knew, would never support conscription and to do so meant delivering Quebec to Henri Bourrassa and his nationalist group. Laurier declined and the stage was set for a political and social confrontation that would split the country along linguistic lines and lead to one of the saddest, and least remembered, incidents in Canadian history.

By the fall of 1917 Borden had formed a union government out of his own Conservatives and Liberals from outside Quebec and this coalition was confirmed in the federal elections of 1917. This election, whose only issue was conscription, bore out the linguistic division of the country. The Conservatives were virtually wiped out in Quebec, gaining only three seats in that province. For their part the Liberals took only 20 of their 82 seats from outside Quebec. When the vote on the Military Service Act was taken some days later, virtually every English-speaking MP in the House of Commons voted in favour and virtually every French-speaking MP voted against the measure.

As the war progressed, domestic issues, such as Rule 17, began to cloud the question of Canada's participation in Britain's war effort. The streets of Montreal and Quebec City were frequently the scene of sizeable demonstrations of pacifist and anti-conscriptionist sentiments, most often led by prominent members of the clergy or members of the nationalist political elite. In March 1918 the protests in Quebec City were becoming louder and more violent. In response to these demonstrations the federal government dispatched troops from Toronto to try and neutralize the crowds. However, their very presence only angered the protesters further. On April 1, 1918, the protests grew increasingly violent as a full-blown riot erupted in Quebec City's Saint-Sauveur district. The riot began with an anti-conscription protest march but soon deteriorated when members of the crowd tried to capture the city's armoury. Overwhelmed by the mob, the troops charged in with their bayonets and then opened fire on the crowd, killing four and injuring many more. The federal government subsequently threatened to impose martial law in Quebec City if the protests didn't end. While the government gained the upper hand after this confrontation, it lost what little support it had in French Canada and further angered its opponents who saw in the Quebec City killings evidence that English Canada was ready to use any means to gain Quebec's compliance.

The conscription question brought out into the open the underlying divisions that existed between French and English Canadians in the early part of the twentieth century. The scars left on the national psyche would remain long after the war and would once again be evident when conscription resurfaced during World War II.

The conscription question highlights a fundamental issue: while French Canada had developed its own sense of nation, that is being Canadian, English Canada had not developed a similar notion of a Canadian identity that would prevail over the British affiliation. While Borden may have dreamed of Canada emerging into its own as a consequence of the war, in fact his political manoeuvrings simply reinforced the notion of the British *mère-patrie*, a notion which excluded all who were not of anglo-Protestant stock. What the conscription crisis of 1917 proved yet again was that the Canadiens had a diametrically different vision of the country. The Canadiens were isolated from France for years and had developed a distinctly "Canadian" identity, while English Canadians still defined themselves and their nationality in terms of the British link.

The conscription crisis was yet another nail in the coffin of the Conservative Party as it was virtually wiped out in the province except for a few minor successes in isolated ridings. The break with the Liberal domination of provincial politics came in 1936 when the Union Nationale, under Maurice Duplessis, was elected for the first time. By this time Quebec's economy was beginning to emerge from the Depression and the future looked bright for Quebec. However, World War II would once again plunge the country into the depths of a national unity crisis.

On September 10, 1939, the government of Mackenzie King declared war on Germany. Right from the outset of the conflict King promised that Canada's contribution to the war effort would be entirely voluntary. In Quebec, Maurice Duplessis won his seat in October 1939 with a pledge to fight centralization and conscription although the Union

Nationale lost power. Meanwhile, politicians in English-Canada were beginning to criticize King for what they considered a half-hearted war effort. To placate these criticisms King decided to call a snap election for September 1940, an election he won handily. King thus had a mandate to conduct the war as he saw fit and for a time his management of the war went unchallenged. However, in 1942 Arthur Meighen returned to federal politics to lead the Conservative Party. Meighen's first act was to run in a by-election in Toronto in February 1942 during which he made conscription his only campaign issue. Challenged once again, King announced in the January 1942 Speech from the Throne his intention to hold a referendum on the issue of conscription. This move by King effectively cut down Meighen's only issue and the CCF won the by-election. However, although King had used the promise of a referendum for plainly partisan motivations, he now had to deliver on his promise and risk alienating Quebec.

A plebescite on conscription was called for April 1942. Even after calling for the referendum, King was determined to keep all his options open. King's government kept the plebescite question vague, asking only for a mandate to free the government from any obligation which might restrain its ability to fill military ranks. In Quebec, the "NO" forces were made up of many of Quebec's future leaders. Men such as Pierre Elliott Trudeau, Jean Drapeau, and André Laurendeau joined forces with Duplessis and his Union Nationale party and Montreal Mayor Camilien Houde to try and defeat conscription.

In the end, the anti-conscriptionists knew they were fighting a lost cause as the weight of English-Canada's electorate was enough to smother, yet again, the Quebec vote. In Quebec the final tally was 75% against the government, while the national vote was 63% in support. "Conscription if necessary but not necessarily conscription" was how King chose to manage the situation after the plebescite. His first move was to ask Parliament to approve the National Resources Mobilization Act (NRMA). The NRMA would enable the government to call men up for home defence but also provide for overseas services "if necessary." However, for some Quebec Members of Parliament the Act was "conscription enough" for them to leave the Government. Other prominent Quebecers were subsequently arrested for their open opposition to conscription. Among the arrestees was Montreal Mayor Houde who upon his release would be greeted with a hero's welcome after the war and later sit in the House of Commons as a member of the Bloc Populaire.

The scenario of 1917 appeared to be playing itself out again. English- and French-Canada were divided just at the moment when Canada's military requirements overseas were escalating. Pressured by his cabinet and public opinion in English-Canada and despite the opposition of his Quebec cabinet members, King approved overseas service for conscripts in 1944. Although a few minor protests occurred in Quebec, overall this final measure was accepted with resignation. With the war nearing its end, very few Canadian conscripts made it to the battlefields of Europe. As it turned out the referendum may simply have created a situation, eventually turning it into a full blown national unity crisis, that was largely over. The divide between English-Canada and Quebec grew a few metres wider between 1942 and 1945 and as historian Desmond Morton suggests, another bitter memory was preserved for those whose motto is *Je me souviens*—I remember.

Quebec under the Union Nationale

While Maurice Duplessis' early electoral successes may have been caused by a profound desire for change in the social and political situation that existed in the province at the time, his years in power proved to be some of the most conservative in the history of Quebec. Under Duplessis the Church was able to regain much of the power and prestige it had prior to 1900 and the traditional elites in Quebec society were restored to their positions of privilege. Progressive elements, especially in the universities and the labour movement, were silenced.

The Duplessis years were marked by a desire to set Quebec on a course of its own. As a result Duplessis vigorously fought every attempt by the federal government to centralize power. In 1947 Duplessis created a Quebec revenue department to collect its own corporate tax, followed in 1953 by the introduction of the provincial income tax. Although largely symbolic, both of these measures were used by Quebec to assert its independence from the federal government. Duplessis was also wary of federal programs such as the Canada Pension Plan that was being discussed while he was in power. Through his refusal to adopt progressive social policy in conjunction with the federal government, coupled with his profound orthodoxy and Roman Catholicism, Duplessis managed to slow the pace of change in the province and thus hampered Quebec's move into full modernity.

The Duplessis regime left many Quebec nationalists in a quandary. While they supported his efforts at preventing federal intrusions in provincial areas of jurisdiction, Quebec's nationalists were increasingly unhappy with the mood of conservatism which prevailed in the administration of the province. Moreover, some expressed displeasure that progressive social initiatives such as Medicare were being ignored by the Union Nationale government. While nationalists concurred with Duplessis that Medicare represented a federal intrusion in provincial affairs, they expected the provincial government to implement its own program. To no avail. Duplessis not only opposed social programs on "nationalistic" grounds, he also opposed them on ideological grounds.

The Quiet Revolution

Quebec proved remarkably resilient and quickly bounced back from this period of social and political conservatism after the 1960 provincial election. Termed the "Quiet Revolution," this period was to have reverberations which are still felt to this day. Most of the issues which are debated in Quebec and Canada today have their genesis in this period and many of Quebec's current crop of politicians, businessmen, academics, and other social leaders grew up during this period.

The Quiet Revolution grew out of the opposition to Duplessis and his policies and was lead by intellectuals and labour leaders, two segments of Quebec's society which Duplessis had tried hard to silence. Magazines such as *Cité Libre* and newspapers such as *Le Devoir* provided the outlets for progressive ideas while the provincial Liberals provided the political machine to defeat the Union Nationale.

Quebec after 1960 underwent rapid change. The educational and social services system were taken out of the hands of the clergy and placed in those of the provincial bureaucracy. In fact, one of the most dynamic forces of change after 1960 was the bureaucracy. It is where Quebec's new class of university graduates soon found a place and where they began to take apart the institutions that they felt had hampered Quebec's development. The new bureaucrats were young, educated and hungry for change as opposed to their predecessors who were less educated and mostly interested in preserving the status quo.

One of the major symbols of the Quiet Revolution, apart from the overhaul of the educational system, was the nationalisation of the province's electric utilities. Championed by then Energy Minister René Lévesque, Hydro-Quebec was created to ensure inexpensive and dependable electricity to all Quebecers and industry. Electric power at low cost was seen, then as now, as one of the key building blocks for Quebec's economy. To this day Hydro-Québec and hydro-electric mega-projects have an almost mythical place in the minds of many Quebecers. In addition, the nationalisation of the electric utilities enabled Quebec to offer tangible benefits through rural electrification programs.

The Quiet Revolution also freed up the nationalist movement in the province. While nationalism was always a political and social force to be contended with, Duplessis and the clergy had tried to control it for purposes other than their own. After 1960, however, the new intellectual and political freedom in the province led many to question the relationship which Quebec enjoyed with the rest of Canada. A genuinely separatist movement made up of nearly a half dozen groups of various political ideologies began to organize in the mid 1960s. In 1967, the issue of Quebec independence caused a split within the governing provincial Liberal Party. Lead by René Lévesque, a faction made up of party members and MNAs moved a motion that would have made sovereignty-association for Quebec the party's first electoral plank. The motion was defeated. René Lévesque and many of his supporters left the meeting and the party. Lévesque formed the Mouvement souveraineté-association (MSA) later that year.

By 1968, the MSA had merged with other sovereignist movements to form the Parti Québécois, a political party whose first aim was to take Quebec out of Canada. Later that same year the left-wing Rassemblement pour l'indépendance nationale, a much larger separatist group, folded in favour of the PQ.

The darker side of the Quiet Revolution emerged on October 5, 1970, with the kidnapping of British diplomat James Cross. In Ottawa, Pierre Trudeau imposed the War Measures Act. Many innocent citizens were arrested and incarcerated without trial. In addition, federal troops were dispatched to guard all federal buildings and other "sensitive" institutions. A few days after the imposition of the War Measures Act the body of Pierre Laporte was found stuffed in the trunk of a car parked in the Montreal suburb of St-Hubert.

The October Crisis dragged on into December when the police finally located the FLQ hideout where James Cross had been kept for nearly 80 days. The kidnappers were promised safe-conduct to Cuba in exchange for releasing Cross and on December 4, 1970, four FLQ members flew out of Dorval airport headed for political asylum in Cuba. In the weeks that followed the FLQ members responsible for Laporte's death were found and subsequently tried and convicted of murder.

The October Crisis had lasted 83 days, but for many Quebecers it was to have a much more lasting effect. In the end 468 Quebecers were arrested without justification; some were imprisoned for as long as 21 days. Yet, not a single person arrested by police during these sweeps was ever charged with any illegal activity. Like the conscription crises of 1917 and 1944, the proclamation of the War Measures Act by the federal government reinforced the negative attitudes with which some Quebecers perceived the federal government. In a political system where reality always seems to come in a distant second to perceptions the federal government was increasingly being painted as a bully to Quebec.

While many nascent political parties would have been irreparably harmed by events such as the October Crisis, the PQ survived. It had successfully rallied the nationalistic forces to its fold and succeeded in getting about 25% of the popular vote in its first election, though it received only seven seats. Before long the PQ would surpass the now moribund Union Nationale at the polls. While the PQ was a definite force to contend with in the streets, in the National Assembly, the party never had more than seven members before its victory in 1976. Even during the October crisis, when one would think that separatist sympathies would have been at an all time low, the PQ still received nearly 30% of the vote in opinion polls.

In the general election of 1976 the PQ finally cashed in on the general feeling of disillusionment which Quebecers had towards the governing Liberals and won its first term in office. The PQ had strategically chosen to put its sovereignty option on the backburner, choosing to run on a good government platform and promising to hold a referendum on Quebec's status before taking any action on the sovereignty issue. Contributing to the PQ's victory was a rejuvenated Union Nationale under Rodrigue Biron. The UN received a disproportionately large share of the popular vote, much of it coming from angry English-speaking Quebecers who turned against the Liberals after the passage of Bill 22, the law which made French the official language of Quebec. Bourassa himself was defeated in his own riding. The next four years would be some of the most exciting in the history of Quebec, let alone Canada.

Quebec under the Parti Québécois

The first PQ government had a progressive bent and in its first years in power introduced legislation in the areas of automobile insurance, the protection of agricultural lands, consumer protection, health services and, of course, language. However, despite these popular measures the real test was still the promised referendum on sovereignty-association. After much debate the Government finally decided on May 20, 1980, as the date for its referendum, nearly four years after coming to power. The referendum question became the object of much planning, discussion, and argument, with the final text being adopted on March 20, 1980.

In the National Assembly the Liberal Opposition, lead by Claude Ryan, demanded a clear wording that would encapsulate the Government's intentions. On the government benches, fully aware that support for sovereignty was on the wane and that a straightforward question on sovereignty would likely not pass, the inclination was towards the ballot question. The result was a text that asked Quebecers for a "mandate to negotiate sovereignty-association." The final wording was decided as much by market research as by politics.

The referendum results were a crushing defeat for the PQ and a personal defeat for Lévesque and Claude Morin, his minister of intergovernmental affairs and chief architect of the referendum strategy. Quebecers voted against sovereignty-association with a resounding 59.9% majority. Lévesque gamely addressed his supporters, concluding aloud that the final results were an unequivocal NON, but then he simply said "next time."

Referendum Aftermath

While most political organisations would have been crushed if their number-one electoral plank was so resoundingly defeated by the people, the PQ came back to win the election of spring 1981. During this mandate Canada would once again be tested by Quebecers. Rather than opt for the staunchly federalist Ryan, Quebecers, happy with the way the PQ was running the province, stuck with Lévesque. While the PQ had again campaigned on a good government platform, it would have to face after its election the irony of being a separatist party mandated by the people of Quebec to sit with the federal and provincial governments to discuss the patriation of the Canadian constitution.

The negotiations did not go well for the PQ government. In the end, the Lévesque Government gave away its long-standing veto on constitutional change in exchange for a deal it had worked out with seven of the other provinces. The basic element of the provincial counter-offer was the granting of a veto on constitutional change to every province. For his part Prime Minister Trudeau fought hard to include in the constitution a guarantee of fundamental freedoms, which became the Charter of Rights and Freedoms in the final constitutional package.

With eight provinces onside, Lévesque was positive he could achieve a constitutional accord that would give him most of what he and the

PQ had tried to achieve in 1980. However, the common front against the federal initiative began to break down shortly after the Supreme Court of Canada ruled that although the federal government had the right to unilaterally repatriate the Constitution, convention suggested that the approval of the provinces was necessary. A final federal-provincial meeting was organized and the political manoeuvring began in earnest. Premier Bennett of BC had ceased to act in concert with his other provincial colleagues in the weeks prior to the meeting and played the role of middleman, relaying messages back and forth between Trudeau and his provincial colleagues.

The alliance that had existed until this point between Quebec and the other provinces broke down at the Château Laurier hotel in the wee hours of November 5, 1981. During this meeting, Saskatchewan's Attorney General Roy Romanow, Ontario's Attorney General, Roy McMurtry, and federal Justice Minister Jean Chrétien met to draw up the outline of a constitutional agreement. Other parties were raised out of their beds to join the talks. Other parties, that is, except Quebec. The result became the Constitutional Act 1982. It included Trudeau's Charter, a notwithstanding clause and an amending formula. Quebec's René Lévesque was presented with a fait accompli when he met his counterparts for breakfast the next morning. The night of November 5, 1981 still lives in Quebec's political lexicon as *La nuit des longs couteaux*, the Night of the Long Knives. The stage was now set for Meech. Quebec, having voted to stay in Confederation the year before, now found itself in the situation of being the only province not to sign the Constitutional Agreement of 1982. Although the final document bears the signatures of three Quebecers—Trudeau, Chrétien, and André Ouellet—it lacked the one that counted to bring Quebec on board, that of René Lévesque.

Lévesque's refusal to sign the Constitutional Accord had little impact in Quebec at the time. Although many in the nationalist circles were angry with the outcome and others who had fought for the "NON" in the referendum campaign felt betrayed by Ottawa's failure to produce renewed federalism, many more were indifferent. In fact, shortly after the ratification of the Accord polls indicated that most Quebecers approved of the new agreement.

As for the PQ, ratification of the Constitutional Act 1982 was seen as yet another defeat, but it offered further proof that the party had to rethink its strategy if Quebec was ever to become an independent state. Claude Morin's strategy of *Étapisme*, or the step-by-step process towards independence, was openly assailed at party meetings. Soon afterwards the PQ's electoral machine and organisation began to fall apart. Senior ministers resigned and Lévesque's leadership was openly challenged from within the party. After months of indecision Lévesque resigned on September 2, 1985.

The party had already begun to split into two factions, one ardently *indépendantiste*—the so-called *pur et dur*—and one willing to work within federal structure but with greater autonomy for Quebec. The latter, lead by Pierre-Marc Johnson, the son of former Quebec Premier Daniel Johnson, eventually won out and Johnson became PQ leader in January of 1985, following Lévesque's resignation. The PQ was defeated at the polls in December of that year by the Liberals under Robert Bourassa.

By this point the established order had already changed in Ottawa. Pierre Trudeau resigned for the second time on February 29, 1984, and was succeeded by John Turner. The general election of September 4, 1984 proved momentous as the federal Liberals were wiped out in Quebec for the first time since the Diefenbaker sweep. With the election of Quebec premier Robert Bourassa and the Liberal party in December 1986, constitutional renewal became one of the Muroney's first orders of business. As early as August 1984, Mulroney had stated his desire to see Quebec sign the Constitution "with honour and dignity." This message, coupled with anger at the federal Liberals, had sent many nationalist Quebecers to work for the federal Conservatives in 1984. It had also motivated a good number to run for office. Even avowed supporters of the "OUI" option in the referendum of four years prior joined the PC machine. Many were elected in the Conservative sweep. When the House reconvened after the election, Quebec's Conservative deputation and members of cabinet had an obvious nationalist bent.

One of Prime Minister Mulroney's highest profile recruits to the federal cause was longtime friend and former OUI campaign organizer, Lucien Bouchard. Bouchard left his private law practice to become Canada's ambassador to Paris in 1985 and later entered cabinet in 1988. Bouchard's oratorical skills soon made him the highest profile Tory member from Quebec. In the meantime another round of constitutional talks had begun. In May of 1986 the Government of Quebec presented what it considered to be its minimum conditions for adhesion to the Constitution. These conditions were: recognition of Quebec as a distinct society; a greater provincial role in immigration; a provincial role in appointments to the Supreme Court; limitations on the federal spending power; and a veto for Quebec on constitutional amendments. In August of the same year all the provincial premiers agreed that the first constitutional priority should be discussions around Quebec's five conditions. Federal-provincial negotiations began soon afterwards and culminated with the April 30, 1987, First Ministers' conference at Meech Lake, Quebec. On June 3, the First Ministers met for an all-night negotiating session at Ottawa's Langevin Building. The result of these last minute negotiations was the Constitutional Accord 1987, or the Meech Lake Accord.

The process of provincial ratification began with Quebec's National Assembly being the first to give assent to the deal on June 23, 1987, one day before Quebec's national holiday, St-Jean-Baptiste Day. However, the Accord soon ran into trouble. New Brunswick's new Liberal government wanted changes made to the Accord. Then, on December 19, 1988 Manitoba's new government withdrew the Accord from the legislative calendar. By May 1989, the dissident provinces numbered three when Newfoundland's new Liberal government also announced its intention to seek changes to the Accord. On November 23, Newfoundland's legislature acted on its threat and voted to condemn the Accord. Newfoundland would fully rescind its support in April of 1990.

By early 1990 the prospects for passage of the Accord looked grim. Premier Bill Vander Zalm was wavering and in Quebec the Liberal party established a committee to consider Quebec's constitutional options in the event the Meech Lake Accord was not ratified. In March of 1990 Premier McKenna presented a series of companion amendments to the Meech Lake Accord. If the other provinces agreed to these amendments, New Brunswick would sign Meech Lake. On March 22, 1990, Prime Minister Mulroney established a Special Committee, headed by Jean Charest, to examine the McKenna proposals. The Committee's unanimous report was presented to the House of Commons on May 17, 1990, and the government immediately acted to include some of its recommendations as a basis for a revamped Meech Lake. For some Quebec members of the House of Commons the Charest Report's recommendations proved more than they could live with. On May 18, François Gerin crossed the floor of the House of Commons to sit as an independent. The previous day, Lucien Bouchard, Minister of the Environment, faxed a letter from Paris to a meeting of former OUI organizers who were marking the tenth anniversary of the referendum. As soon as the letter was read to the gathering, a political storm erupted in Ottawa. Mulroney's longtime friend was preparing his exit.

On May 22, Lucien Bouchard returned from Paris and announced his resignation. As he left 24 Sussex Drive following a private talk with the Prime Minister, he argued that the Charest Report was a betrayal of the Government's promise to Quebec. On May 23, speaking before the Montreal Chamber of Commerce, Lucien Bouchard announced that he would stay in Parliament and work towards Quebec's independence. Over the next year seven Members of Parliament would join the ranks of the Bloc Québécois. An eighth would join the group after winning a by-election in Montreal in August 1990. By August 1991 the BQ numbered nine with the defection of Pierrette Venne, whose motion to redraw Canada's internal boundaries was laughed off the floor of the Conservative Party's annual convention. More defections were rumoured, though none ever came.

In the interval, despite a last minute meeting held in Ottawa in June 1990, the Meech Lake Accord foundered and then died. In Quebec, the death of Meech was seen by many as the final straw. English-Canada had humiliated Quebec once again. On June 23, 1990, Premier Bourrassa went on Quebec television to announce his government's response to the failure of Meech. Bourrassa ended his tersely worded statement with a tough message for English Canada: "Quebec is, and will forever be, a distinct society."

CHAPTER SEVEN

A Short History of Western Canada

The history of the West within Canada is similar to Canada's colonial past in the British Empire. The West, and the Prairie provinces in particular, has been a captive market to the industrial heartland situated in Ontario and Quebec. Westerners have been, in large measure, political slaves to the "national" agenda set by Ottawa—a national agenda which was really the regional agenda of Ontario and Quebec. Unearthing the history of western Canadians' political and economic relationship with the rest of Canada reveals the sources of the present mindset and psyche. History also reveals the reasons underlying Western Canadians' squeamishness towards the "national" musings of Ontario and Quebec.

The nucleus of the politics of Western suspicion of the East began around the turn of the century. This suspicion was due largely to the policies of the federal government that favoured the economic structures of the East. The policies not only dealt the West blow after blow, but were incapable of being receptive to Western grievances nor were they able to constructively change for the better. Therefore, the reservoirs of resentment have been allowed to build up and now pose a threat to Canada's unity.

Early Regionalism
As the Western provinces modernized, the sense that the West was developing into a region unto itself increased. Economic cross-pollination and immigration would contribute significantly to a common and positive definition of the West by Westerners. At the same time, political and economic subservience to the East was creating a negative definition of an alien Canada vis-à-vis the West—in other words, Western regionalism. Business and trade in the West caused the region to think and compete in regional terms. Although Eastern banks, farm equipment companies

and retail chains like Eaton's permeated the West, Western companies created links within the West. Alberta's Burns Meat Packers, various insurance companies based in Winnipeg, and British Columbia timber companies spanned across the West.

Even in British Columbia, where the Rocky Mountains acted as a natural barrier to trade and business, strong economic ties with the other Western provinces soon developed. The Prairies created what BC historian Jean Barman describes as an "inexhaustible" demand for British Columbia wood. In fact, by the 1910s two-thirds of BC's lumber was shipped by rail to the Prairies, although the wood was shipped to lumberyards owned by BC lumber companies. These companies in turn sold their products to Prairie residents. The Prairies reciprocated. By the 1920s, 40% of the wheat grown on the Prairies was sent through the port of Vancouver. Although trade links between BC and the Prairie provinces were quite strong, the same cannot be said of the trade ties between BC and Ontario, Quebec, and Atlantic Canada. These trade links, when they existed, were minimal at best.

Early economic ties brought not only business, but people and ideas from across the West in contact with each other. Economics therefore helped foster a shared Western identification. Immigration is another factor which led to the creation of a positive Western heritage of which Westerners could be proud. The entry of masses of new Canadians and their settlement in the Western provinces injected Canada with a refreshingly new understanding of what Canada was about.

Immigration is perhaps the most significant factor in the development of a regionalist view of Canada. Beginning in 1896, under the Liberal minister of the interior Clifford Sifton, wave after wave of new Canadians poured into the Prairies. Immigration figures showed immigration to Canada increased from 16,835 in 1896 to 272,409 in 1907. Until the start of the World War I Canada received at least 140,000 new Canadians per year and as many as 375,756 and 400,870 in 1912 and 1913. Lured by the promise of free or cheap land, the overwhelming majority of these immigrants settled in the Prairies. In the span of forty years, the West's population went from about 4% of Canada's total population in

1881, to over 28 % of the total in 1921. Saskatchewan by this time was Canada's third largest province.

To survive on the Prairies the members of different ethnic groups had to cooperate with each other. The harsh climate also reinforced among Westerners the importance of their community. Essentially, they could beat the odds, such as drought or ridiculous CPR rates, by helping one another. This gave many Westerners a sense of autonomy, a sense that they could go it alone without depending on anybody or anything except their immediate community.

The Eastern elites and establishment reacted to these ideological and philosophical challenges to the established order by referring to these as treasonous or un-Canadian. The irony of course is that these new notions were homegrown alternatives to those adopted from Britain. Over time these new ideas found a foothold in Western Canada. The West had become, in many ways, a social and political laboratory and it is from this laboratory that vibrant and modern ideas about Canadian society and the nature of the Canadian federation emerged.

A vastly different view of Canada developed amongst Western settlers. Most of the new Canadians had no ties to the East and they soon developed a Western view of Canada, a view which would profoundly shape their identity as Canadians. This was the foundation of a broad Western regionalism, spanning across the Prairies and later into British Columbia. These Canadians began to see their country through regional eyes, based on regional concerns. Many of the East's obsessions, like French-English relations, were non-issues in the West. Even Ontario's obsession with maintaining the British link was looked upon with curiosity by most Westerners, except for British Columbians. Although the Eastern establishment tried to drag Westerners into its petty pre-occupations, Westerners increasingly distanced themselves from them. It was the East which seemed provincial, with its Old World baggage in this new land.

Western Canada's most significant contribution to Canadian political and social thought is the notion of regional politics. The very notion of regional politics clashed with the conservative notion that prevailed in

Eastern Canada in the early years after Confederation. Yet, when one looks at the issue critically, one cannot but conclude that Macdonald's National Policy had regional politics at its heart.

Later on, Manitoba entered Confederation on unequal and insulting terms. It even became the butt of jokes in the East. The Liberal leader of the Opposition, Alexander Mackenzie, said in the House of Commons that "The whole thing has such a ludicrous look that it only puts one in mind of some incidents of *Gulliver's Travels*. It is one of the most preposterous ... schemes ever submitted to this legislature."

Subsequently, Wilfrid Laurier was not at all prepared to bargain in good faith. In fact, Laurier was prepared to dictate the terms of Confederation. On February 21, 1905, legislation for the creation of Alberta and Saskatchewan went before the House. In the end, both provinces entered into Confederation in 1905 as unequal provinces. As with Manitoba, Ottawa would keep control of mineral resources and crown lands in their best interests, a decision which would cause some grief between Alberta and the federal government many years later. The creation of two provinces and the granting of only a quasi-provincial status to them, fit into the colonial mindset which prevailed in Ottawa at the time, an outlook which the politicians in Ottawa shared with the establishment in Southern Ontario and Montreal. Rather than maximizing the potential of Alberta and Saskatchewan in and of itself and in Canada, Laurier limited it. Perhaps as a final irony, in an act of historic pettiness, Laurier did not invite Frederick Haultain, the great Western statesman and the person behind the push for province status for the Northwest Territories, to the ceremonies marking the official creation of Alberta and Saskatchewan.

The West before World War II

If Ottawa treated the Western provinces as colonies, then Eastern business kept the West as its vassal. The National Policy ensured that the West would remain captive to the East. National interests and unfair freight rates milked the Western agricultural producer of capital.

Sir John A. Macdonald's National Policy is taught in most history books as a bold economic strategy formulated for the good of Canada and which was responsible for bringing Canada into the modern industrial age. Instead of reciprocity, or free trade, with the United States, Macdonald's Conservatives devised a plan to create an internal Canadian market for goods to support Canadian industrial growth. It is generally acknowledged that it economically solidified what Macdonald had tried to politically accomplish with Confederation.

The National Policy consisted of these three components. First, a railway connecting Eastern Canada to British Columbia was to be built. It had been a condition for BC to join Confederation, but it also served to open up the West to colonization. Second, settlement of the Western provinces was to be encouraged for two reasons: to secure the West against possible American aggression by populating it. and a populous West would provide a captive market for goods manufactured in Eastern Canada. The third facet of the National Policy was the establishment of a tariff wall so as to protect internal markets for a small but growing industrial core based in Ontario and Quebec.

To many, the National Policy may have been the best option for Canada. However, it made the West, from BC to Manitoba, effectively a colony to the East. In the minds of many Westerners the National Policy subjected them to economic exploitation and inequality. For example, a feature of the railway was that there was no alternative route. Its users had no other choice of transportation and were thus captive of whatever rates the railway saw fit to charge. The rail companies did indeed take advantage of the situation. They charged unfairly high prices to Westerners, with Ottawa's full approval.

In fact, the freight rates charged by the railway in 1887 were so exorbitant that they led Manitoba Premier John Norquay and his Conservative government to try and find an alternate route. Norquay's proposal was for a provincially funded rail link to the American border. The Manitoba Red River Railway would provide an alternative to the monopoly of the Canadian Pacific Railway. This plan was quickly crushed by Ottawa. Using his foreign contacts in New York and London, Prime Minister Macdonald sabotaged the bond sale that would have raised the capital needed to begin construction. Further, through the Lieutenant-Governor, Macdonald spread rumours, probably false, about Norquay's involvement in financial irregularities. Norquay resigned within two months, his plans leaving with him.

Prairie wheat and other staples continued to be transported for processing and to market via the Canadian Pacific Railway. The Prairies would be kept a captive market by Ottawa and the legendary CPR, (immortalized by such writers as Pierre Berton as a symbol of Canadian unity) , and soak Westerners for everything it could.

Another aspect of the National Policy, tariff barriers, made it impossible for farmers to purchase cheaper foreign tractors and other farming implements. As farm machinery manufacturer Massey-Ferguson boomed, Western farmers bore the financial brunt of a 35% tariff on farm equipment. This tariff would later increase. This was extremely difficult for farmers in a very competitive world marketplace.

Effectively, the National Policy created a captive market in the West, but on the East's terms. The West was to produce primary resources, while the East sold its finished goods to the West at prices determined in Toronto and Montreal. Thus, wheat farmed in the West was not processed in the West but in Toronto and Montreal. This same flour, alongside expensive farm machinery and textiles made in Montreal or Toronto, would be shipped back to the West for a sale at huge prices. The National Policy satisfied the financial and industrial ambitions of Ontario and Quebec, but not the ambitions of the nation as a whole.

The National Policy was, in fact, far from *national*. In effect, Macdonald had created the first government initiative steeped in regional politics, that is, the regional politics of Ontario and Quebec policy. Meanwhile, many Westerners paid for Macdonald's "national" ambitions with their money and labour. As Randall White suggests "... the problem with John A. Macdonald's old National Policy was not that the federal government should avoid any kind of exercise in national development strategy. It was only that the old National Policy was the wrong national policy. The right one would work for all regions, not just for Central Canada."

The issue of the freight rates charged by the CPR to the residents of the

West also stirred Western anger, as evidenced in Premier's Norquay's bold attempt at building another railway. As early as 1883, when the Canadian Pacific Railway published its first freight schedule, the West would be at the CPR's whim. Like the national government, the Canadian Pacific Railway discriminated between two classes of citizens: Westerners and Easterners. The people of Ontario and Quebec were provided with freight shipping costs at about half the cost per mile of those provided to Westerners. Almost as if to exacerbate the growing split between East and West, Manitobans paid a higher rate than residents of Ontario and Quebec. The people of Alberta and Saskatchewan paid a higher rate than Manitobans and British Columbians paid the highest rate per mile of all Canadians. This unfair treatment would grate on the nerves, not to mention the pocketbooks, of Westerners until the 1950s. Looking for justice, Westerners brought this blatantly discriminatory practice to the attention of Parliament. The response from Ottawa was that the CPR rates represented "fair discrimination." Needless to say, this did not restore the faith of Westerners in the federal government.

Bad policies aside, what the National Policy or the CPR demonstrated was that the vestiges of British-style colonialism were evident within Canada, rather than in some faraway land. The elites and the population in Ontario and Quebec felt comfortable with these paternalistic ideas and allowed them to continue in public policy and in economics. For over a century, until the signing of the Free Trade Agreement, the legacy of colonialism would remain. Until then, Western frustration would result in outbursts of anger and protest.

By the 1890s and early 1900s Westerners were beginning to say enough was enough. Across the West, Canadians had decided to rid themselves of Eastern oppression to make better lives for themselves. Drawing on their history of self-reliance, the same quality that had permitted Westerners to prosper on the sometimes unforgiving prairie, Western Canadians began to take action. This action took two distinctive paths. Western Canadians began to join together in political protest. This would lead to the rise of the United Farmers Party, the progressive movement, and the Co-operative Commonwealth Federation (CCF). Westerners would also look to their provincial governments to protect them from the East.

The Winnipeg General Strike of 1919 was one demonstration of the frustration which permeated the West. On May 15, 1919, twelve thousand workers from the primarily Eastern-owned factories walked off the job. To the organizers' surprise, the factory workers were joined by thirty thousand more workers from all industries. The strike sparked similar walkouts in other cities, Vancouver among them. The strike lasted just over one month, by which time the federal government had had enough. Seeing in the strikers the early risings of a Bolshevik revolt, Ottawa ordered the Mounties to end the walkout. The strike leaders were arrested in dawn raids and by June 21, the strike was all but over. However, on that same day thousands marched to Winnipeg City Hall to protest the arrests. The Mounties charged into the crowd with clubs in an event that would go down in history as Bloody Saturday. The Winnipeg General Strike re-enforced the distrust which many Westerners had of Ottawa and it further led to a durable alliance between the labour movement and socialist politics.

Other populist movements would rise as Western Canadians began to show their dissatisfaction with Central Canada. These movements, like the Winnipeg strike, arose out of the frustration Westerners had with unfair freight rates, the West's entrapment through the National Policy, and basic economic exploitation at the hands of eastern Canadian interests. Moreover, Westerners were becoming increasingly skeptical about the ability of both the Liberals and Conservatives to articulate the interests of their region. Populist political parties would rise to challenge the Liberals and Conservatives especially after the Conservatives stuck to Macdonald's National Policy and, after failing to win an election based on reciprocity with the United States in 1911, the Liberals joined the Conservatives in supporting the National Policy. This left many Westerners with little choice but to support a new party.

In the 1920s the Progressives moved out of nowhere to become the second largest party in the House of Commons. This party accomplished little in the way of direct change because of internal divisions. What is more, the Progressives failed to deliver the provincial equality and economic fair treatment that Canadians in the West needed. Sadly, the distrust and anger Westerners had towards Eastern Canada were therefore allowed to fester. If the Progressives had a positive effect, it was that they served notice to the Conservatives and to the Liberals that the West's concerns would be represented, with or without their involvement.

Province Building

By the outset of World War II, provincial governments were becoming essential to Westerners' sense of security vis-à-vis the East. In the interwar period they had been used as an anti-East bastion through which Westerners were able to get important concessions from Ottawa. For the first time, through their premiers, Westerners were able to bring the West's problems to the attention of the nation and get something done about them. For example, the federal government finally gave the Prairie provinces control of their natural resources in 1930. This occurred mainly because Western provincial governments had forced Ottawa's hand. By trying to provide the same infrastructure, schools, telephones, and roads, for their residents as those enjoyed by other Canadians, Alberta and Saskatchewan almost went bankrupt. The provinces certainly were assured of no help from Ottawa. Despite deriving no money from their natural resources, Alberta, and Saskatchewan decided to go ahead with these capital projects. Faced with two almost bankrupt provinces, Ottawa finally relented and ceded control over natural resources to the Western provinces in order to get itself off the hook. But by no means did that challenge Eastern hegemony.

The Premiers would become *the* voice of the West against Ottawa. In essence, Westerners gained a form of effective regional representation in Ottawa and tried to stand up to the more powerful East. This form of regional representation would really become most effective after the World War II, and especially under Lougheed, but at this point it was just beginning to take form.

The Depression in the 1930s had a profound effect on the relationship between provincial governments and provincial residents. After years of poor treatment from the East, the provinces offered services and protective legislation helping Westerners.

The Depression cemented the role of the Western provinces in the lives of Westerners. Before the Depression, the West had been badly hit by many cyclical downturns. Westerners were used to being vulnerable to economic changes and severe weather. These cycles were part of the reason many Westerners banded together to ensure a secure livelihood. However, the Depression was different. It hit the Prairies harder than anywhere else in Canada because of a combination of a ten-year drought and a collapse of the world wheat market. Between 1928 and 1932, the average income dropped by 71% in Saskatchewan and by 61% in Alberta. What aid Prairie Canadians could muster came from one another or from their provincial governments.

What little federal assistance there was, was resented by many Westerners. Meanwhile, Eastern banks, with their large two-storey Greek facades dominating Prairie towns, were cutting their losses and retreating to a safer East. In contrast, Westerners banded together and helped those in greater need. From Carmen, Manitoba, to Calgary, Alberta, the better off would have food waiting by the back door when a hungry neighbour or stranger discreetly came asking for help. The governments of the Prairie provinces also established a number of programs in an attempt to make life easier for the residents of their provinces. For example, the Alberta Social Credit government placed a moratorium on the collecting of farm debts. It also established the Treasury Branch banks, giving Albertans banks that would not leave the province and, moreover, were run by the Albertans for Albertans. The provincial government showed itself to be receptive to the concerns of the people and in the process of implementing basic social reforms, the provinces gained much legitimacy.

By the outbreak of the World War II, western Canadians had learned two valuable lessons. First, the East could not be trusted to make an honest commitment to Western Canada, especially in tough times. Second, Westerners realized that the only path to change lay in their hands, through the likes of populist political movements and especially through their provincial governments. After the war, these lessons guided the next generation of leaders and thinkers towards a confident new West.

The Post-War Years

After World War II, Canada experienced an extended economic boom. With the exception of industrialized Ontario, a branch plant of the United States, and Quebec, the boom was primarily resources-driven. Most provinces, but especially those with abundant mineral wealth, timber and fossil fuels, prospered by feeding the American industrial machine with primary goods. With jurisdiction over mineral deposits, the governments of western Canada grew in importance. By charging royalties, provincial governments increased revenues which, in turn, enabled the provinces to provide their residents with security, strong public works, and an educational infrastructure. They attempted to diversify their economies away from resource extraction. The Western provinces were the leaders in implementing innovative changes to social programs. In 1948, for example, Saskatchewan came up with a universal medical program, later copied by the other provinces. British Columbia, which had considered public health care as early as 1936, soon followed suit, as did Alberta, albeit with a free enterprise twist. Like other provinces in Canada, the Western provinces developed excesssive public education systems. In Alberta, this meant a massive expansion of post-secondary education. The University of Calgary and the University of Alberta grew tremendously and technical institutions such as the Northern Alberta Institute of Technology and the Southern Alberta Institute of Technology sprang up overnight, or so it seemed.

At the same time as Westerners were busily building and attempting to diversify, Ottawa, Toronto, and Montreal continued to threaten the West with indifference. Ontario and Quebec were still the economic and political centres of the country, and they wallowed in their prosperity. It didn't seem to matter to central Canada what the rest of the country was doing. The East continued to produce consumer goods for the nation behind an artificial tariff wall, while the West supplied resources.

In 1960 Alberta pressed Ottawa for the creation of a national oil pipeline, extending from Alberta to the refineries of Montreal. The offer gave the East the opportunity for a constant supply of Canadian oil. Moreover, it would bring a boost to Canadian production. The proposal was the sort of good faith and good business gesture needed to build a true North, strong and free. A myopic Ottawa retorted that it was cheaper to import the oil from Venezuela. At the beginning of the oil crisis in 1973, Alberta extended the offer once again. Federal Energy Minister Donald Macdonald repeated the same line. Not making Alberta's oil available to the whole nation was in the national interest. Venezuela was cheaper. Ironically, less than ten years later, the Liberal government would demonstrate that the "national interest" was equally as cheap.

The National Energy Program marked a new page in the history of western Canada and demonstrated to Westerners that the colonial mindset evident in Macdonald's National Policy was still very much alive in Ottawa. If the East could not exploit the West indirectly and systematically, it would without hesitation do it directly. The West's worst fears were sadly realized. However, this was not the same West as one hundred years earlier. It was a very new and modern West—one which had a strong sense of itself. Westerners were both proud of what had been accomplished and secure in the knowledge that they could make a prosperous living, largely on their own. Moreover, unlike their forebears of one hundred years earlier, the provincial governments were much stronger. Provincial governments had a legitimacy, as providers of services and defenders of the interests of the Western Canadians, that the federal government did not have. In addition, these governments were led by aggressive new leaders like Peter Lougheed who were demonstrating that, unlike Ottawa, they would be looking out for the West's long- and short-term prosperity. In contrast, Ottawa and the eastern business community had only proven to be self-interested, as they had been a hundred years earlier. The Trudeau government's National Energy Program, created at the behest of Ontario and Quebec, would drive a wedge between the East and the West. The divide separating the West from the East would grow wider.

Many of Trudeau's policies had a major impact on Canadians in the West. These were the product of a Government without any substantial Western representation and with what seemed to Westerners to be a general air of arrogance and disdain towards them. By 1980, only two Liberal MPs, both from Manitoba, represented the West on the Government benches. From 1980 to 1984 not a single Liberal Member of Parliament held a seat west of Winnipeg. Trudeau himself queried the western grain farmers, "Why should I sell your wheat?" He also became famous for his one-fingered salute to Westerners. Trudeau and his Liberal government were completely out of touch with the West. They implemented policies as if it were not part of the nation, to exploit it for Eastern purposes. Initiatives such as the implementation of the metric system, the National Energy Program, and the Foreign Investment Review Agency, as well as the patriation of Canada's Constitution, were interpreted in the West as assaults on their region. Instead of making initiatives in a truly national vein, Trudeau effectively pandered to the economic interests of Southern Ontario.

For the second time in one hundred years prosperity in the Western provinces was stunted in order to keep the economic engine of Ontario, and to a lesser extent Quebec, running. The National Energy Program, like Macdonald's National Policy, left an indelible mark in the minds of many Western Canadians. The NEP made it possible for Ontario to enjoy cheaper oil while at the same time taxing one the West's most vital resources. University of Calgary economist Robert Mansell estimates that between 1960 and 1986 the NEP cost Alberta almost 60 billion dollars. Even former Liberal Energy Minister Marc Lalonde acknowledged that the NEP was more political than practical; designed primarily to satisfy the government and people of Ontario, it succeeded in this goal at the cost of an alienated West.

What made the NEP so glaringly wrong to Westerners was that Alberta had acquired ownership of its resources with full provincehood in 1930. When oil companies drilled for oil, they were drilling for oil which belonged to Albertans. The government of Alberta sold this oil to companies and Alberta generated revenues in the form of a royalty. The money generated from the sale of this non-renewable resource was either reinvested in diversification programs or bankrolled in the Alberta Heritage Trust Fund. However, instead of supporting Alberta's good fortune, the Eastern establishment looked enviously at the massive revenues generated from oil production in Alberta. Wrapping themselves in the national flag, Easterners, and southern Ontarians in particular, pushed for a cheap oil strategy. The government of Ontario proposed, in a white paper, that Alberta oil be sold to Ontario at prices less than world prices. This, it was suggested, would be done for the national good. When, fresh from an election victory, Trudeau launched the NEP, the spectre of the National Policy was raised all over again. Combined with the limits of the freedom of foreigners to invest imposed by the Foreign Investment Review Agency, FIRA, and the meddling in the West by an Ottawa-owned oil company, PetroCan, the NEP had distinctly colonial qualities.

Alberta Premier Peter Lougheed's condemnation of Trudeau's power grab was swift. Oil production was immediately cut to a minimum and Alberta's government launched a legal challenge into the constitutionality of the NEP. All the Western premiers chimed in with their support for Alberta. Popular reaction in the West ranged from sober, sad dismay to outrage. In the West the NEP was blamed for everything from increases in the suicide rate to the rise of Western separatism. Trudeau had opened up old wounds that would not be healed easily. The rift between West and East grew wider. Disillusioned, Western Canadians began to re-explore structural reforms to Canada.

Some advocated massive decentralization of the country. Other Westerners suggested that the needs of Canada could be served through putting a regional balance in Ottawa. The political and economic status quo became clearly, and totally unacceptable.

The Progressive Conservative government of Brian Mulroney came to power in 1984, and was re-elected in 1988, in large measure because of Western support. The federal government went quite far to ease regional alienation, especially the fear of further official exploitation of the West by the East. For once, with ministers such as Don Mazankowski, Harvie Andre, and Joe Clark, the West finally had strong representatives in cabinet.

One of the new government's first measures was to toss out the NEP. In addition, a Western-oriented regional development agency was established to assist with the West's diversification. Most significantly, the new Tory government threw out the last formal vestiges of the National Policy by entering into a Free Trade Agreement with the United States. The removal of the tariff walls and the limitations placed on government involvement in the Free Trade Agreement made it impossible for the East to use the West as a vassal again.

The Reform Party, formed under the banner "The West Wants In," began to capture some Western impulse towards structural change. Initially the Reform Party was an unconventional political party in as much as its platform was not based on policies, but on institutional reform, in particular a Triple-E Senate—effective, equal, and elected. Other political parties such as the Alberta provincial Conservative party and the three other federal parties, began to get on the institutional reform bandwagon, though to varying degrees. The message of structural reform has therefore spread throughout Canadian politics. It has become a Western necessity in all further constitutional change. Now we have the Alliance Party under Stephen Harper. The Alliance Party continues to be in trouble. Even if it disappears altogether, it would be wrong to conclude that the problem of Western alienation has been solved. The opposite is true.

New Beginnings

Today, the West feels as confident and sure as it ever has. Westerners are well educated and set to take on the new economic challenges that the world is offering. Trade in the Pacific Rim has enormous potential. Already, BC's trade with Asia equals that of its trade with the United States. In the arts community, directors like Anne Wheeler, best known for her film, *Bye Bye Blues*, and musical groups like Spirit of the West, are exuding the energy of the new West. In fact, the West is giving Canada new ideas, new means of expression, and new business. Many Westerners look optimistically to the future.

By exploring the history, politics, economics, and cultural evolution in Quebec and the West, I truly believe we can help liberate positive forces that can bring us together in a new and meaningful way. It has been said,

"We do not know our strength if we do not know our history." Do we, as Canadians, really share a common view and appreciation of our history? I think not. Yet our shared past should give us strength go a long way to uniting our citizens and regions in a new and fulfilling sense of Canadianism.

CHAPTER EIGHT

The Power of the Finance Department

Our next government and future prime minister must radically reform the budget process and bring the department of Finance and its officials under control. The elected representatives of the people, including cabinet ministers, are normally consulted and have some input into government legislation. However, the powerful Finance department is immune to this general rule. Budgets and other measures have been finalized by officials and announced by the Finance department without public debate or consultation, and without reference to cabinet or the government's parliamentary caucus. By any standard, democracy suffers as the people's representatives lose control of the purse strings. Our next prime minister must be ready to radically reform the budget process and the manner in which the department of Finance functions.

In the last half of the twentieth century, a number of politically charged measures involved the department of Finance and the Bank of Canada. For example, Walter Harris, Louis St-Laurent's Finance minister, just before the 1957 election announced a paltry increase in the old-age pension of six dollars per month, handing John Diefenbaker an issue for the campaign trail. During the Diefenbaker years, Don Fleming, Diefenbaker's Finance minister, got into one fight after another with the provinces, notably Newfoundland and Term 29. While Fleming was overly combative and partisan, he was also badly advised by officials at Finance. Then there was the Coyne affair and the devaluation of our dollar during the 1962 election campaign. Between 1963 and 1984, disastrous budgets crippled government.

After I was sworn in as minister of state for Social Programs and Science and Technology in 1979, it didn't take long for me to realize that Finance wielded unlimited power. Much to my surprise and, at times, indignation. Finance officials sat in on cabinet meetings and even cabinet committee meetings, representing the minister and speaking on his behalf. It became all too clear to me that the Finance department enjoyed privileges denied other ministries. What was worse, it was immune from cabinet scrutiny and caucus debate—enjoying an immunity denied other ministries and their departments. To understand how such fundamental rules of democracy could be broken, we must look back.

"No taxation without representation" constituted a central theme of the people's claims as parliamentary democracy evolved in Britain. The same principle was heard in the American colonies in the 1770s.

To be taxed only by duly elected representatives became hallmarks of most of the legislative institutions in the free world. The most important means by which Parliament rose to its historic position of supremacy was the power of the purse.

The Stamp Act of March 1765 made trouble for Westminster in Britain's North American colonies. Americans had to buy stamps of various kinds, ranging in price from a few pence to several pounds, to be placed on different classes of legal documents and newspapers. The British could not have imposed a more unpopular measure on the American colonists. H.C. Allen wrote in his book *A Concise History of the USA:*

> Deeds and mortgages relating to property, licenses to practice law, licences to sell liquor, college diplomas, playing cards, dice, almanacs, and calendars all had to bear British stamps of stated values. More than this: publishers and printers of advertisements, newspapers, and other sheets had to buy stamps for their publications. If the British Parliament had deliberately searched for taxes that would annoy as many Americans as possible, it could scarcely have improved upon the Stamp Act.

Lawyers and merchants were quick to voice their resentment against it. The cry "No taxation without representation" was taken up in cities, towns, and the countryside by artisans, mechanics, farmers, and housewives. Popular societies called the Sons of Liberty and Daughters of Liberty were organized. Crowds gathered in the streets of Boston, New York, Philadelphia, and Charleston and rioted against officers who tried to force people to buy stamps. The offices and houses of royal officials were stoned and in some cases sacked and burned. Going far beyond blocking the sale of stamps, Americans organized groups to boycott British goods. There was so much disorder in several colonies that even the protesting merchants and lawyers became frightened and tried to restrain the torrent of popular anger. Eventually, in 1766, the Stamp Act was repealed, as control of the purse strings and taxation by the people in the colonies was considered paramount.

How ironic it is that successive auditors-general have informed Parliament and the Canadian people that our legislators have lost their ability to control the purse strings effectively.

Harold Laski, in *Parliamentary Government in England* (1938), tells us:

> Finance is not something apart from policy but an expression of it. By deciding what to do in other spheres, the House largely decides by inference what it is to do in the financial sphere.

In Canada today, budgets far surpass throne speeches in importance and few, if any, government initiatives escape the influence of the department of Finance.

One of the notions that has weakened our present-day Parliament's control over the nation's purse strings is the continued belief in budgetary secrecy. In the United States, many budgetary provisions are given advance publicity so that public debate can take place. Although no one should be able to gain financially from being privy to advance information about budgetary intentions, there is still no excuse for the crippling secrecy that surrounds budget-making within the Canadian Parliament. Even the former mandarin Mitchell Sharp came to this conclusion after serving as Lester Pearson's Finance minister, and told me as much in conversation.

It is arguable that the devaluation of the Canadian dollar during the 1962 election cost the Diefenbaker government many seats. It was done in the middle of the campaign, without full cabinet approval or parliamentary debate. In December 1982, during a meeting at York University, I asked Bob Bryce, formerly a deputy minister of Finance and clerk of the Privy Council, why budgetary measures were prepared in such secrecy. Bryce cited the danger of advance leaks and the disconcerting effects that these might have in international markets. Little was said of the fact that over the centuries, the power of the purse had passed from the hands of despotic kings into the bowels of an entrenched, unresponsive bureaucracy. You can cut kings' heads off, but bureaucracies are hard to personalize; individual public servants are more often than not civilized and decent people who do not appear to have sinister intentions.

Bryce went on to say that by and large, budget considerations and proposals are very complex, so that it is often hard to explain them clearly to cabinet ministers and members of Parliament. Several business executives were present at our conversation. They reacted with consternation, knowing what would happen in the private sector if senior officials of a company could not give clear and understandable explanations of policy direction.

Canada is not alone in its inordinate preoccupation with budget secrecy. The Dalton case in Britain's post-war Labour government is a classic example. A supplementary budget was to be introduced at Westminster because of mounting financial difficulties in the country. On his way to the House of Commons, Hugh Dalton, the Chancellor of the Exchequer, passed a reporter in the lobby, and they briefly discussed some aspects of the proposed budget. Minutes before Dalton began reading his budget speech, *The Star* came out with headlines reading "Penny on Beer, Tax on Pools and Dogs Likely." Dalton had been a loyal member of the wartime cabinet, so Churchill was very conciliatory as leader of the Opposition, not pressing for an immediate resignation. However, Churchill asked that a select committee investigate the affair. The next morning, Clement Attlee and other cabinet colleagues tried to dissuade Dalton from resigning, but after Churchill's demand for a select committee became known, Dalton tendered his resignation and it was accepted.

By the time I was appointed parliamentary secretary to the Finance minister George Nowlan in the summer of 1962, the Diefenbaker government had already been rocked by successive clashes with the governor of the Bank of Canada, James Coyne, and by his decision to devalue the dollar in mid-election. Donald Fleming, the former minister of Finance, liked nothing better than partisan confrontation, and Finance officials were only too glad to supply him with ammunition.

Between 1963 and 1984 the federal department of Finance, normally distant from political reality, was at the centre of three disastrous budgets and the defeat of the Government on a money bill.

Before the 1963 election, soon-to-be Finance minister Walter Gordon repeated time and time again that a new Liberal administration would usher in a legislative program that he called "sixty days of decision." The "sixty days" slogan was a phrase borrowed from John Kennedy's first weeks of office in the United States—sixty days of action referred to the period just after Kennedy's election. Gordon's proposals were hastily prepared and ill-conceived.

Heading this series of blunders was Gordon's first budget, presented on June 13, 1963. In fairness, officials of the department of Finance cannot be blamed for it. Gordon's relations with his deputy minister Kenneth Taylor were cool, to say the least. The minister had called upon outside advisers, mostly from Toronto, to help him prepare his budget. The fact that he had relied on outside advice was revealed only after persistent questioning in the House by Doug Fisher, the NDP member for Port Arthur. As Gordon was valiantly attempting to pilot some of his budgetary provisions through the House, my colleague George Nowlan called me over in the Commons chamber and pointed out that none of our old friends from the Finance department were in the officials' gallery. This gallery is normally reserved for senior public servants who wish to attend debates when matters affecting their ministry are being discussed. Senior mandarins can quickly pass advice down to their minister and be immediately in touch with general proceedings and developments. Irked at Gordon's decision to hire outside consultants, most senior Finance officials boycotted his budget speech and the subsequent debate. The carpet was being gently pulled from under the feet of an idealistic new cabinet minister.

As a nationalist, Walter Gordon advocated measures that he felt would encourage the indigenous economic growth and ownership of Canada's economy. He met strong opposition within the cabinet, especially from Mitchell Sharp. Ken Taylor had no sympathy for Gordon's views, since Canada had to attract foreign capital, especially from the United States. Eric Kierans, a fellow Liberal, publicly called Gordon's budget foolish and unrealistic. Even if many of Gordon's economic goals were laudable, his hurriedly cobbled-together proposals were not feasible or attractive to voters. Yet what contributed most to his downfall was that he had worked in secret.

Eventually most of Gordon's proposals were withdrawn or modified. He had fallen at the starting gate, never to recover; his reputation and party standing were in tatters. While he did not immediately resign, this initial disaster was a prime factor in his eventual departure from the Finance portfolio. Most influential Liberals saw him as an impetuous maverick.

Budgets can bring down more than ministers. The headlines in many papers across the land on February 20, 1968, read "Liberals beaten 84-82." Mike Pearson, who had announced that he would be stepping down as leader and prime minister, was in Jamaica, and his party was in the throes of a leadership race. On the night of a Commons vote deputy prime minister Paul Martin, Sr. and two Liberal backbenchers were in Trois-Rivières for a leadership campaign meeting. After the defeat of the Government bill to raise taxes by imposing a 5% surcharge on personal income tax, Bob Stanfield called on the Government to resign. NDP leader Tommy Douglas said that if the government tried to restore its position in the Commons by asking for a vote of confidence, his party would oppose it. The whole procedural fiasco was a terrible embarrassment for Mitchell Sharp, who had leadership aspirations of his own. It was he who had presented the Government's bill.

Robert Winters, the Trade minister and the number-three man in the cabinet pecking order, quickly summoned an emergency meeting of senior ministers. He, too, had leadership hopes and wished to minimize the damage to himself as the man in charge. Such learned fellows as Eugene Forsey offered convoluted constitutional explanations to suggest that the minority government could carry on despite the fact that it had been defeated on a money bill. Pearson hurried back from the Carribean, but it was clear that the cabinet was deeply divided on the best course of action to take.

On February 21, Pearson was lustily cheered at his party caucus. We held our own caucus at the same time and claimed that the Government had no right to stay in office. Stanfield decided that the Conservatives would boycott committee meetings. Pearson faced an angry Opposition and challenged it by presenting a tough but complex confidence motion. Pearson asked the Commons to vote that its defeat of the Government's tax increases would not constitute non-confidence in the government. The debate was slated to start on the following Friday, and I began to sense a slight softening in the Opposition's stance. Although I have never thought that we should blindly follow British constitutional precedent, I could not help thinking of Westminster during this parliamentary turmoil. It is unlikely that such an amateurish mistake would have happened there, but if it had, the Government probably would have been more contrite and the Opposition more bullish. Yet in Britain they never keep one party in power for very long, and no single party gets infected with the "divine right to rule" disease.

I thought that there were several political risks in precipitating an election during the Liberals' leadership race, but did not entirely appreciate the advice that Stanfield was given by Finance department officials. They told him that the defeat of the tax measures would do incalculable damage to Canada at home and abroad. Their advice made Stanfield more cautious, and he said that he would not allow a filibuster during the Commons debate. I often wondered if the decent and statesmanlike Stanfield realized he was being counselled by many of the same advisers who said that we must devalue during the 1962 election campaign.

Réal Caouette declared he would oppose the Government, but a few days later he changed his mind, saying that he had lost faith in both the NDP and Conservatives. Gordon Churchill quit the Tory caucus to sit as an Independent Conservative because the party was caving in. Earlier in the week, our caucus had agreed to allow the Government motion to come to a vote without filibuster. That meant that the Government was off the hook and that the 84-82 vote against its crucial tax bill was not a vote of non-confidence. Churchill felt basic principles were being violated, and he had many allies on our back benches. He wanted to go for the jugular and go to the people.

The vote took place on February 28. Only one Tory, who had been ill, failed to appear, and the Liberals won by 138 to 119. Two things saved the day for the Grits. Pearson rushed back to the Commons from overseas and rearranged the order paper putting the money bill, for the time being, on a back burner. Secondly, Stanfield and his troops backed off. The Grits survived, unlike the Tories when Diefenbaker and Clark squandered their minority governments. It is for the reader to guess what would have happened if, after the Government was defeated in the House, we had gone to the people. Would Pierre Trudeau ever have seen the light of day? Maybe not.

Only after sixteen years in opposition would we finally get our chance again. I had the honour to serve in government with some excellent cabinet colleagues; with time, I thought that we would become an effective administration. Soon after I was sworn in to the cabinet as minister of Science and Technology I came to realize that while ministers must master their own portfolios, they court disaster if they do not understand the workings and powers of the Prime Minister's Office, the Privy Council Office, the Treasury Board, and the department of Finance. While the prime minister, then Joe Clark, would have been the first to accept the blame for our defeat in the House and ultimately at the polls, once more the Finance department largely contributed to our downfall.

Cabinet documents are normally supplied to ministers before meetings of cabinet committees so they can assess the political implications of decisions that may be taken in the full cabinet. The only minister who escapes these procedural requirements is the Finance minister. He, his deputy, and the prime minister, and sometimes the clerk of the Privy Council, are really the only people who are fully briefed on the import of the budget before its final form is put before the House. This tradition has exacted an unnecessary political toll and will continue to do so until the whole question of the budget's preparation is reformed. Budgets usually have grave political implications. The fact that they are formulated with no proper political vetting seems incredible. No amount of prior consultation with interested parties can begin to replace parliamentary control over budget-making.

John Crosbie's budget of December 11, 1979 might seem in retrospect quite a statesmanlike document, but for a minority government just getting under way, it was political Russian roulette and bravado heavily sprinkled with a good dose of subliminal Tory masochism. The proposed changes would affect the capital-gains tax and help farmers and small businessmen, but nobody on the Opposition benches noticed that or talked about it. An immediate excise tax on gasoline was what did it: the tax at the gas pumps was all I heard about in every corner of my riding during the ensuing election campaign. The fact that the Liberals subsequently compounded the felony does not seem to have mattered. The Conservatives were about to lose power. When we finally went down on prime-time television, I made no apologies for having lost my cool in public during an interview on the French-language network in the lobby of the Commons, after the vote.

In my view, Clark's failure to save the day and continue on in government constituted the single greatest error in political judgement in the history of Canada.

Few people can claim the title "a House of Commons man." Stanley Knowles and John Diefenbaker were two who could. To obtain such recognition requires an intuitive sense of the House and its peculiar moods. Allan MacEachen was also a superb parliamentarian who knew how to parry and thrust when the going got rough, with an uncanny debating style and knowledge of the rules of the House. He almost single-handedly engineered the collapse of the Clark government in December 1979. It is hard to imagine a man with such astute political instincts becoming entrapped in the labyrinths of the Finance department. Yet that was the case when he presented his second budget on November 12, 1981.

Admittedly, it was not entirely the fault of the senior mandarins in Finance. At a time when the economy was in the doldrums and when the private sector needed stimulus, MacEachen presented an astonishing budget. The minister's left-of-centre views, instilled in him during his days at St. Francis Xavier University, the spiritual home of the Co-operative Movement, were just not suited to the times. Officials at Finance worked overtime, poring over the flow charts. It seems that they were preparing a budget for another country, at another time, and in another world. Provisions to help farmers, developers, and small business just would not fly. Deferred annuities were to be hit hard. If enacted, these provisions would have seriously crippled Canada's insurance industry, as noted; subsequently, they were to be largely and conveniently ignored.

The Canadian Tax Act is unnecessarily complex compared with those in other Western democracies, and MacEachen's blunderbuss attempt at tax reform proved to be a disaster. During my years on the Hill, no budget suffered more from public opprobrium than MacEachen's second effort. Most of its central proposals were withdrawn or ignored; the minister's reputation as a superb political tactician was left in shreds.

Conventional wisdom has it that those who accept the Finance portfolio are digging their own political graves. If that is true, it is not because the minister often has to initiate unpopular measures. For the most part, the public would understand that. It is because the minister invariably has to do so within the framework of outdated procedures, cloaked in secrecy. He is denied the capacity to take the necessary soundings of the House and the country. How else did such stalwarts as Fleming, Gordon, Crosbie, and MacEachen bite the political dust?

In April 1982, MacEachen issued "A Paper on Budget Secrecy and Proposals for the Broader Consultation" to try to allay public criticism. Leaders of labour and industry in the private sector and politicians and government officials in other departments affected by Finance's extensive power cried out for immediate reform. MacEachen had to move.

MacEachen's paper was intended to stimulate the public discussion necessary to lead to modification of the tradition of budget secrecy. Some background observations make interesting reading. Ministers in the past had had much to say. Walter Gordon observed, "The old established tradition—according to which budgets are prepared in the department of Finance, without consultation or discussion with other officials or outside experts, and without informing the cabinet of what is going to be proposed hours before presentation to the House—should be changed."

In 1969, Edgar Benson, minister of Finance, stated, "What I would like is for the minister to be able to present a tentative basis of his proposal to Parliament for discussion. The way it is now, the minister of Finance has to present highly important advice from a very small group of expert advisers in a form which the government can understand, and on this the government stands or falls, and I think this is wrong."

Donald Macdonald, in his budget speech of May 1976, expressed this sentiment: "The time has come to consider whether some of the long-standing traditions that surround the budgetary process should be modified to serve better the needs of today." He added: "Two aspects of the budgetary process require particular study. The first is the strict rule of secrecy that applies to the budget prior to its introduction. The second is the procedure for consideration of the budget proposals following their introduction in Parliament."

The Honourable John Crosbie stated in 1979: "I hope it will be possible in the coming session of Parliament to examine the entire process of budget-making. We could begin by referring the entire area to a committee of the House of Commons."

MacEachen's paper underlined the necessity for creating a more open pre-budget process: "The original concept of budget secrecy was relatively narrow: to protect against financial advantage or gain." However, he went on, "the tradition inhibits consultations within the government. The recent introduction of the government's expenditure management system has greatly expanded the need for extensive interdepartmental and interministerial discussions in the pre-budget period." Moreover, "the extreme interpretation of budget secrecy does not take account of the broad economic and social role which modern budgets must play." MacEachen concluded that "a redefinition of budget secrecy is necessary to ensure that broader consultation and a more meaningful response to pre-budget submissions from the public are possible."

The paper suggested that consultative bodies be established, and that a permanent advisory committee be set up, consisting of outside tax specialists, to provide advice on a regular basis to the minister of Finance and his officials. The Canadian Tax Foundation recommended that a permanent tax-reform commission be established independent of the Government and Parliament.

MacEachen's paper also noted:

> The redefinition of budget secrecy would contribute to an improved framework within which public consultation in the pre-budget period could take place. Other positive steps would be for a minister of Finance to issue green papers, white papers, or other less formal documents providing information on certain policy or technical issues that he wanted to address in a future budget. This would inform those with a particular interest of expertise that an area of tax policy was under consideration and enable them to make representations before final decisions are taken. The release of background papers on certain policy initiatives or technical changes that are under consideration also would undoubtedly serve to improve the two-way communication process. This is particularly so in those complex areas of the law where the government cannot be expected to have all the information necessary for a full assessment of the impact of proposed changes.

MacEachen recommended the idea of a regular date to present the budget each year; such scheduling would overcome the uncertainties that now exist and would allow for an organized preparation of the budget. A fall date was suggested.

We should never forget that the budget is a political document and that therefore changes must take place in the House of Commons itself. The executive should retain decision-making authority, but members of Parliament themselves should define and determine the political climate.

Past studies of the budget process have underlined two basic problems: there is insufficient opportunity for broad debate on major initiatives of taxation policy, and there is insufficient opportunity to correct technical deficiencies in tax legislation.

Many people have recommended that the secrecy rule be amended. The one recommendation that must be acted on immediately is that all taxation bills in draft form should be submitted to a standing committee of the House of Commons for clause-by-clause scrutiny.

What most governments lack is a feeling of the mood of the country, which Parliament normally accords to the legislative process. As James Burns and Timothy Denton wrote in a paper on the budget process:

> The practice initiated in the June 28, 1982, budget of referring complex proposals to outside experts for technical analysis is an excellent one. These individuals are not asked—nor would their training and non-political backgrounds compel them—to comment on the political philosophy or advisability of a proposal. Their task is to translate a government's stated policy objectives into legislation and regulations which will most effectively achieve what is desired.

This is an important consideration. Many ex-ministers have told me they would never have presented certain legislation to the House if they had realized how much subsequent regulations and interpretation would ruin their original intentions for the legislation.

In my view, the pre-budget debate should be focussed in public hearings before a special committee of Parliament, and the department of Finance's forecast of the economy in the coming year should be the *raison d'être* of the debate.

Undoubtedly, the department of Finance must be the dominant economic portfolio. I well remember the constructive role its officials played when, as minister of Science and Technology, I weighed the pros and cons of increased tax incentives for industrial research and development. On the other hand, it is imperative that we get the debate about the budget process out of the rut of secrecy in which it is now mired. A better budgetary process is one precondition for restoring to Parliament its traditional rights of proper control over the purse strings. The reward for the country will be incalculable.

More recently, the Finance department and its minister, Paul Martin Jr., have shown extreme insensitivity to the erosion of our health care system. When waging war on the government deficit and cutting and reducing transfer payments to the provinces, without consultation, no provisions were made to safeguard the basic workings and principle of Medicare.

The immunity of the Finance department and its officials from political realities and grass roots concerns once more has done much damage. The painful results are there for all to see. Our next prime minister must immediately reform and update the budget process, otherwise history will, sadly, repeat itself.

CHAPTER NINE

Where To Now?

As I review the history and the concerns that I have discussed in this book, I recognize that I represent a type of Toryism that many people do not even know about anymore. For many years I represented the riding of Brome-Mississquoi in the Eastern Townships of Quebec. My heart lies in the seasons and landscape of this spectacularly beautiful part of Quebec. In that natural setting perhaps it makes more evident good sense to preserve what is worth preserving and to change what needs to be changed—the essence of Progressive Conservatism.

The Native people are right: we receive our environment from those who went before. We pass it along to those who follow us. I am profoundly troubled by changes in the climate and other components of the ecosystem in which we live.

We are mesmerized by the fast-evolving electronic networks that are permeating our lives. Yet we cannot ignore our roots. Our natural heritage and our democratic traditions are precious legacies. It is our responsibility to pass them on. When I talk with people I visit in the Townships and across Canada, I recognize that my political agenda reflects their bedrock values.

The Progressive Conservative Party of Canada has fewer than 15,000 members. The majority of federal constituencies do not even have local executives democratically elected by party members. The party is millions of dollars in debt. The party of Macdonald and Cartier is hived off on the Opposition side of the House of Commons with twelve members, in fifth place, after the Liberals, the Alliance, the Bloc, and the NDP. This is a disgrace that should never have happened. Yet, even in the face of these negative circumstances, I firmly believe that the Progressive Conservative Party can form the next Government. The challenge is great but it must be met if my party and its members are to fulfill their individual and collective obligation to Canada and its people. Forming the next official Opposition should never be our goal. Voters want to vote for a party that will form the Government that will effect changes they ask for. They want to *win* their vote.

Before the last election, Joe Clark said he would ascertain if we would run candidates in every riding from coast to coast. When the writ went out calling the election, we had, at most, nominated 20% of our candidates. The other 80% were nominated a month or so before the election. It takes time to build a profile, and they had absolutely no chance of winning. Most party members wonder what the leader has been doing since he gained leadership of the party four years ago.

After the last federal elections I sent Joe Clark a letter with specific recommendations for organization of the party at the federal level, with copies to the Tory caucus. He never responded. To win the next election the party needs drastic re-organization. Party offices must be opened immediately across the country for the purpose of organization and fund-raising activities. By July 1, 2003, 350,000 new party memberships must be sold across Canada, averaging a thousand new members in each riding. The riding party executives must be duly elected by the party membership. Early in 2004, open and well-publicized party conventions must be held in every riding coast-to-coast. At these conventions party members must name excellent winning candidates, ideally ten months before the election date. This would give the PC candidates time to work and organize before the next election is called, and guarantee them victory at the polls.

There is much work to be done at the local constituency level—the success of an election depends upon this. (See Appendix: Campaigning to Win). Through the local constituency level we can bring Canadians back into the political process. In Quebec there are only four elected riding executives. Clark has shut down the Montreal office—the only one in the province. There are similar stories across this country.

I received a thought-provoking letter from Senator Brenda Robertson that comments on the disaffection with politics all political parties face:

I have believed for some time now that parties are losing their importance in our political system largely because their relevance to ordinary people is on the decline.

Increasingly, you hear that it is becoming more difficult to convince people to join political parties, let alone attend poll meetings or annual meetings. There are many reasons for this. Too many people see politics as a nasty business. Many believe that no one political party has all the right answers. But, I believe the most important reason is simply that young people today, in our fast paced society, are too busy with the daily demands on their lives to get involved with a political party. And even those who make the time to get involved, because they may have a higher commitment to public affairs, have less loyalty to a particular party than we have.

The Edmonton Dilemma

The party's national convention is to be held in Edmonton at the end of August 2002, where the delegates will decide if and when, to have the next leadership vote. The party's fate will be decided in Edmonton. Either we make a decision to take power or a decision will be made by default that will, in effect, diminish the party as a federal force the next time Canadians go to the polls.

I understand Clark's ambivalence about encouraging a leadership vote. He was badly mutilated by the Mulroney forces in Winnipeg in January 1983 and thereafter. Only if Joe Clark encourages a renewed leadership vote with over 300,000 card-carrying members voting, will a Progressive Conservative ever have a chance at becoming prime minister again.

Why do I use the word "dilemma" in describing the Edmonton meeting? It is anticipated that about 1,500 party members will be in attendance. They are and will be individuals who, for the most part, can afford over two thousand dollars to be there. Most of the 15,000 or so card-carrying party members will not be present. Expenses aside, in order for a riding to send delegates to Edmonton, the riding must have a duly elected executive and meet other basic requirements. I estimate that today only 30% of our ridings have duly elected executives.

Low-income people and students will not be in Edmonton. Most workers who staff the polls and get out the vote on election day cannot afford to go. These people richly deserve the right to affect the decision, one way or another, relating to a renewed leadership vote.

The gathering in Edmonton, as of now, will be elitist in nature. That the gathering will recognize its responsibility to the party and Canada is my fervent hope. Something tells me good sense will prevail, that something will happen to eradicate any death wish some party members might entertain. A collective survival instinct will emerge that will resonate with what many Canadians are feeling.

When I drew up the "one member-one vote" recommendation for the party in the mid-eighties, we had approximately 400,000 signed up members. We should have at least 350,000 new members in order to elect a leader in early 2003. This will give a leader a stronger mandate to go forward. We must put an end to our elitist structure. After the leadership vote, we can recruit new members to make sure there are, at a minimum, ten workers for every polling division in Canada when the next election is called. The people are out there, waiting for us to provide leadership.

The next objective will be to have the best possible candidates named in each riding, ideally one year before the next election is called. This requires the party membership in each riding to elect an executive that will convene a nomination convention, with advanced publicity, so that the party membership may elect and name a winning candidate. Local candidates must be democratically elected by party workers. This has been a key factor in my seven electoral victories in Quebec. During all this time, fundraising activities will be stepped up and, with a viable organizational structure, the party will project policies giving Canada and Canadians a new and exciting vision.

The Progressive Conservative name constitutes a well accepted "brand image." Canadians at large consider our party the only reliable and viable national alternative ready to take over from the Grits. They will be ready to vote for us, if we do the right things and get down to work.

As things stand now, the meeting in Edmonton is weighed in Clark's favour. However, something relatively dramatic must happen before the meeting. This could involve a massive party membership recruitment. It could also involve individual Progressive Conservatives declaring their intention for leadership. This latter development would answer those who say, with a shrug of the shoulder, "Who is there to replace Joe?"

Soundings have been taken from coast to coast and Canadians overwhelmingly believe that next August in Edmonton party members should call for a new leadership vote. We would do well to listen to the people.

Broad Policy and Leadership

I wish to spell out what I consider to be a short list of policy concerns that should preoccupy our next prime minister. Party members may easily add to my list of concerns. None of these issues are currently being addressed by the Government. The result of one-party rule in Canada means that substantial issues are being forgotten by an arrogant government and prime minister, who feel they will automatically return to power.

In preparing policy for the future, any opposition party has its work cut out. It is crucial to convince the public that the party has broad policy principles as a basis to form a government. On the other hand, it should not permit policy issues to be stolen by the government in power. Recent history gives us some stark reminders of this dilemma. The governing Pearson Liberals stole the issue of Medicare from the New Democrats. Stanfield, in opposition, was defeated in the 1974 election on the issue of wage and price controls. The Trudeau Liberals went on to enact wage and price controls soon after coming to power in 1974, and so it goes.

It is a problem to live up to party responsibilities by drafting policy initiatives for governing without having them stolen by the party in power. Nevertheless, the dilemma must be faced and solved. Many people and the press in Canada and the United States talk about the "vision thing." I believe a dynamic new leader for our party, one who can clearly articulate policy issues, could offer Canadians a real vision for the future.

These are some issues that should constitute files on the desk of our next prime minister:

Regional Ministers. Mackenzie King succeeded in having strong regional ministers with high national profiles. I think of Macdonald in Atlantic Canada, Lapointe and St-Laurent in Quebec, Howe in Ontario, and Jimmy Gardner in the West. Our next prime minister would do well to emulate King in this regard—delegating real power and authority to strong regional ministers with high national profiles.

The Bureaucracy. During my time as minister, one of the things that concerned me was the quality of cabinet documents prepared by the bureaucracy. Each night, ministers would leave their offices with briefing books to be studied before cabinet met the next day. Most of the documentation was overly long and not that well prepared. It is my guess that this leads to many ministers not reading their briefing papers at all. They arrive at cabinet unprepared and the quality of their participation is severely compromised. I invariably sensed a strong bias in the documentation. Let us say there was a choice to be made between the two types of trucks for the armed forces. It would seem, on the part of the bureaucrats involved, that the decision was already made. Cabinet ministers would be given the honour of choosing the shade of paint for the vehicles.

The next prime minister's transition team must assure that the civil service becomes responsive to ministerial directives and to legitimate public demand.

A number of ministers of the Liberal regime have told me that the central thrust of their legislation was seriously distorted and changed after the relevant act was passed by Parliament. Bureaucratic regulations are the means of this interference with Parliament's will.

People wrested power from despotic rulers as democracy, freedom, and parliamentary government slowly evolved and were established. Now, in the western world, we have largely replaced despots with an unresponsive, unrepresentative, and ever-expanding bureaucracy that has virtually run out of control. The problem lies with bureaucracy as a collectivity; most individual federal civil servants are decent individuals. Yet, when citizens contact them they are "on another line," "have just stepped out of the office," "are out of town" or in one of those interminable meetings that Ottawa is so good at putting together. Reform is necessary to humanize our bureaucracy and make it more responsive. It is also important to ensure that the West and the East are better represented in our nation's capital.

Health Care. The Chrétien government could be defeated on the single issue of health care. Paul Martin cut transfer payments to the provinces without consultation. While his efforts at deficit reduction were laudable, he not only failed to consult the provinces, he failed to consult his own health minister. The reduction in transfer payments obviously had a negative effect on our, heretofore, world-class health care system. Failing to protect our national plan constitutes, in my view, a callous disregard for the health of our people. Restoring and updating our health care system should constitute the most important domestic priority for our new prime minister. Open and equal accessibility to health care services for all Canadians should be the basic principle. Canadians want this. It is one of our core values.

Parliamentary Reform. The balance of power in our parliamentary institutions must be restored without delay. Outstanding Canadians are and will continue to be reluctant to seek a seat in the House of Commons under present conditions. I speak with members of Parliament of all parties. They tell me that the prestige of being elected to the Commons wears thin when the elected MP realizes he or she also has no power at all when it comes to the formulation of policy. Apart from having a voice in caucus, they want real powers to formulate and influence policy. This means more power for members of Parliament and parliamentary committees. It also means more free votes, especially on issues that don't lend themselves to partisanship. members of Parliament should not have to tolerate being named to parliamentary committees, just as toddlers are put in playpens, to get them "out of the way." Our future prime minister must transfer some of the authority now residing in the Prime Minister's Office and Privy Council Office into the hands of individual MPs and parliamentary committees. By so doing, the principle of responsible parliamentary government will be protected.

Question Period. Question Period in the House of Commons has, over the years, evolved into an unproductive shouting match. Like other members, I felt embarrassed when high school students from my riding visited the Commons and watched their legislators in action. Admittedly, in many ways, politics is a partisan blood sport. Even so, there is no excuse for the nature of our Question Period.

Rather than the unstructured procedure now followed, written notice could be given to the prime minister and ministers relating to questions to be asked. The Speaker, after the answer has been given to the initial written question, could also allow one or more additional supplementary questions. The prime minister should attend Question Period on one or two pre-determined days each week. These changes in procedure would not eliminate all disorder during Question Period, but it is to be hoped they would improve on today's unacceptable conditions.

One day after Question Period, the prime minister stopped by my desk in the Commons to congratulate me for the detailed answers to questions put to me. Often in the past, I noted government ministers would take questions on notice to reply at a later date when they had the information. My initiative regarding "idiot cards" meant that I would rarely take questions on notice and this generally improved the atmosphere in Question Period. Here is what happened. Once a week, I would gather a number of officials in the department to brief me on questions. This not only prepared me for Question Period but it also involved many officials in my department in the operation. It constituted a morale boost for the officials and helped me keep on top of my department. I would keep my idiot card index on my knees. When a question was put to me, I quickly pulled out the card having to do with the subject matter involved and was thus able to give a full answer.

Blind Trusts. During the Trudeau years, the rules regarding conflict of interest and blind trusts were put into place. Michael Pitfield, Secretary of the Privy Council, was largely responsible for the blind trust rules. When a vote comes up in the Commons, ministers and members, if they feel they are in conflict of interest, should merely declare their interest and abstain from voting in the Commons or participating in cabinet debate.

After my re-election in 1972, I personally made an inventory of my assets and liabilities and had them verified and certified by a local chartered accountant. My next step was to make an appointment with Al Fraser, the Clerk of the Commons. Fraser, an old friend, gladly took my declaration and filed it. When I boasted and alluded to the fact that I felt my declaration constituted a pioneering initiative, Fraser said this was not the case. He told me I was second in line after Tommy Douglas. The NDP leader had already made a similar declaration.

Blind trusts create much trouble both for the bureaucracy and federal ministers who are obliged to put their assets in such a trust to be administered by officials other than themselves during their term of office. I do not wish to be cynical, but I believe that trusts are not always totally blind. Ministers get a peek from time to time. I much prefer the simple and uncomplicated act of declaring assets and liabilities and depositing the declaration with the Clerk of the House.

Ownership Democracy. The present government is doing next to nothing to encourage entrepreneurship among Canadians, especially our young people. Tax policy and bureaucratic red tape discourage those wishing to start up their own business. Bureaucratic control and interference must not be allowed to dampen the spirit of entrepreneurship. Government should encourage a culture that promotes and produces achievement-oriented risk takers. Government must encourage and promote an "ownership democracy." Democracy is well served when Canadians, living in freedom, have an ownership stake in their country. This means more good, small business persons owning their own businesses, more families owning their own homes, more Canadians investing and sharing in Canadian enterprises, and more good farmers owning good farms. This is a core Progressive Conservative value.

Defence and Foreign Affairs. Since the end of World War II our military and defence establishment has slipped into disgraceful disarray. Morale is low among our troops. Canada cannot live up to its defence commitments within the NATO Alliance. Our capacity to defend our borders and sovereignty has been seriously compromised. Our current involvement in Afghanistan has stretched the capability of our armed forces to the limit.

In foreign affairs, Canada has had a long tradition of being an "honest broker" with a capacity to explain and minimize friction between other powers. Lester Pearson's intervention in Suez speaks for itself. I do not believe, at the present time, being a self-satisfied honest broker constitutes a foreign policy in itself for Canada. When I attended the United Nations General Assembly in 1965, U.S. diplomats told me that President Johnson was more or less boxed in when it came to recognizing China. They said it would be helpful if Canada came out for recognition. After consultation with my party leader in Ottawa, I issued a press release calling for Canadian recognition of China. I surely don't want to exaggerate the effect of my communiqué. It took a few short years before Nixon recognized Mainland China. U.S. bureaucrats thanked me for my initiative, which I hope was helpful even in a very small way.

Our next prime minister should announce Canadian support for a Marshall-like Plan for the developing world. The Marshall Plan for Europe was an imaginative post-War initiative involving great states-manship. Religious differences play a large role in the cleavages relating to the developing world but equally important are the economic disparities between the rich and poor nations of the world. To achieve long term benefit, education and health care should be at the centre of our help, taking care not to not put resources, money and otherwise, into the hands of corrupt leaders who block the assistance going to people at the community level. Cooperation with the UN and our NATO allies constitutes a potential initiative in such a plan. Canada has a major role to play.

The Dollar. The 1962 federal election was largely a one-issue election when Finance minister Fleming pegged the Canadian dollar at 92.5 cents U.S. "Diefendollars" flooded the country during the election and the Tories lost over a hundred seats. A similar "Chrétien-Martin" dollar could flood the country when we next go to the polls. The state of the Canadian dollar should be a prominent file on our next prime minister's desk. The present government must decide whether or not to use the Bank of Canada reserves to protect our dollar or peg the dollar at a fixed rate. One thing is certain: Chrétien and Martin cannot hide behind the independence of the Bank of Canada. The government must act responsibly and act soon to protect our dollar.

A Customs Union with the United States. The United States is by far our largest trading partner. Two-way trade over the U.S.-Canada border is huge. Billions of dollars are wasted by delays and red tape at the border. Protecting our national identity was at the heart of the Free Trade Agreement in the late 1980s. We can anticipate the same debate when it comes to a customs union with the U.S., especially if questions of immigration and security are involved. However, globalization of the world economy is a fact of life. A customs union with the United States is possible, without compromising Canada's sovereignty.

Poverty and Education. The crisis facing our unemployed young people constitutes a national disgrace. Much of the infrastructure of our country is crumbling before our very eyes. Bridges, buildings, roads, waterways and reservoirs require repairs and improvement. Just as the Diefenbaker government addressed winter unemployment with a Winter Works Program, surely, today, the federal authority, cooperating with the provinces and munici-palities, can put the unemployed in general and our young people in particular back to work, giving them hope and letting them share in the Canadian dream.

While education is a provincial responsibility, surely the federal authority has a leadership role to play. Transfer payments to the provinces must assure that provincial governments and local school boards have the funds to upgrade our school facilities and the teaching profession.

Research and Development. In a letter to Joseph Priestly in 1790, Benjamin Franklin wrote, "The rapid progress science makes occasions my regretting that I was born so soon. All diseases may by some means be prevented or cured not excepting even that of old age, and our lives lengthened to beyond the antediluvian standard." Franklin, of course knew nothing about the tremendous strides that have recently been made in gene technology, but he most certainly would recognize the value of research that would, sometime in the future, lead to the abolition of diseases such as Alzheimer's, multiple sclerosis, and certain cancers.

Past governments have promised to increase funding for research and development in Canada. Research and development should produce greater long term prosperity for our country. Yet our record has been bad. The federal authority has continually killed the goose that lays the golden egg. To add to this state of affairs, much of our research in the past has been put on the shelf only to be developed and commercialized by other countries. Compared to other advanced national economies, our federal research and development spending has been abysmally low. This must change.

Intelligence Briefing. A recent headline noted "PM Left out of Intelligence Loop." Under current conditions, this obviously is just not good enough. If the President of the United States gets daily intelligence briefings, surely the same should hold true for our prime minister. At present, intelligence briefings to our prime minister are on a hit-and-miss basis. Additionally, the prime minister must be willing, most of the time, to provide intelligence briefings to Privy Counsellors on the opposition benches and to heads of opposition parties in order to get parliamentary approval for initiatives based on intelligence reports.

The Environment. Environmental protection is always near the top of the public priority list for Canadians. Clean air, water, and soil are rights not be denied to present and future generations. I do not believe that economic expansion and environmental protection constitute mutually exclusive goals. The knee-jerk reaction and confrontation between environmentalists and certain business leaders must end. Admittedly, some economic sacrifices will be necessary as we reach for clean air, water, and soil standards. If these sacrifices are weighed realistically in public debate, I am convinced that environmentalists and business leaders, working together with government, will meet the challenge.

Negative Politics. Our future leader must turn his or her back on negative politics in campaigning. Admittedly, politics constitutes, at times, a sort of open warfare. On the other hand, partisanship should not mean the kind of negative politics we have seen, especially in the United States, during recent years. No wonder voter turnout has dwindled while public cynicism, more than ever, has been directed at politics in general and politicians specifically. Negative politics often portrays, in a vicious and personal way, the character and performance of individual politicians. The truth is invariably discarded as television, radio, and newspaper advertisements go on the attack.

Canadian leaders must once and for all renounce this practice.

Leadership
Will Jean Chrétien stay on for another election? If Chrétien steps down, the Liberals are in for a nasty and divisive fight. Their leadership vote will be based on the old traditional convention rules, open to dirty tricks and all the rest.

If the Progressive Conservatives and Clark do the right thing, a leadership vote based on a one member-one vote rule will be a major factor in paving the way to power. A leader voted in by party militants at the grassroots level means Canadians would have the first government "of the people" in our nation's history. It is my sense that Joe Clark wants to hang on. Let me be explicit. My suggestion for a leadership vote involving 350,000 signed up party members in no way constitutes an attack on our current leader. If Clark encourages such a vote, runs and wins, he could be our next prime minister. If his leadership is confirmed, he will find in me a loyal supporter as I was in the past election. However, if the party decides to choose someone else, our next leader must have experience in elective office, experience as a federal member, and a broad vision for Canada.

Edmund Burke's famous letter to his electors in Bristol, England, has often been quoted. He tells us, with reason, that an elected public official in a free and democratic society can never be just a rubber stamp for public opinion on any given issue at any given time. Character and leadership demand more than that. Leadership by opinion polls is no leadership at all. Trusting the people will not open up the floodgates of mindless populist anarchy. Trusting the people means the end to all the undemocratic notions of paternalism and elitism that often plague our government.

The Progressive Conservative Party of Canada must, once again, become a viable national force, so that the electorate will have a real choice of national parties. In the next few months the party and its leadership must take decisions that will renew the Party and and coalesce Progressive Conservative ranks across the country. Unless we act now, one-party rule will continue in Canada.

Campaigning to Win

The late Honourable George Hees was John Diefenbaker's highly successful Transport minister and, subsequently, minister of Trade and Commerce. He was an indomitable campaigner and knew how to win. A war hero, he was a highly motivated politician who loved going into political battle. In the mid-1950s, before I decided to run in Brome-Missisquoi, I came across a document prepared by George. It was entitled, "Campaigning to Win." Many of my own successful campaigns were based on George's ideas. These are some of his ideas that I have adapted for my own political campaigns.

1. The candidate should have a great sense of public service, and be a highly motivated self-starter with a desire to win.
2. The candidate should be nominated well in advance of the election being announced giving him or her lots of time to get the job done. Ideally, the election should be won before the writ goes out. The actual campaign should only put the icing on the cake.
3. The candidate, once chosen, becomes responsible for the riding organization and party membership. Each riding should have a minimum of one thousand signed-up members.
4. An organizer-in-chief should be named to motivate regional organizers and individual poll captains, and a financial director should be chosen.
5. Poll captains are the key to victory, responsible for the canvassing of individual electors and getting out the vote. Checking poll lists is a must. Lists should be checked by election day.
6. A personal note from the candidate accompanied by national and local party literature should, ideally, arrive at each voter's home before the weekend prior to voting day.
7. When necessary, transportation should be available at the polling

division to get voters out and to the polls.

8. The candidate should delegate fundraising operations to one competent individual.

9. A director for media relations and the distribution of party literature should be named. Careful attention should be paid to the electronic and print media in the riding—daily and weekly newspapers, radio and television. This is very important in rural and small-town areas. Timely and professional press releases should be distributed to the media, after inviting them to special riding events such as the riding nominating convention.

10. Direct mail and outdoor signs and posters should be created by professionals. A good slogan is often helpful.

11. Strategically-located committee rooms should be rented and staffed at the beginning of the campaign.

12. Certain visits by the candidate should, for example, involve town mayors and councils, community organizations, and religious leaders. While these visits are of great importance, the most important is the candidate's personal door-to-door canvass of individual homes.

Ideally, each day the candidate should visit at least a hundred homes over a five- to six-hour period. If nobody answers the door, the candidate could leave a signed card: "You were not in when I called, but I hope our paths cross soon." Try to avoid visits at suppertime and call it a day around 8:30 p.m. As much as possible, be cheerful and rested. Most of this canvassing should be done before the election is called—over a period of eighteen months, completing five hundred visits per week should make for a total of 39,000 completed visits. Visits to businesses and public institutions such as town halls, community centres, and libraries should ideally be done during the campaign itself.

Factory visits during the campaign are essential. Shaking hands with workers outside the factory gate or at the punch clock when the worker arrives on the job is the best way. The candidate should never go to the punch clock when the worker is leaving the job. He or she is normally rushed. If the factory is small and the owner or foreman accompanying you is friendly to your cause, visits inside the factories are possible.

However, this often proves to be inconvenient and a disturbance for workers and management alike. An alternative is to place a sign in the shape of a ballot, on the sidewalk near where you are standing.

MEET

JONES, MALCOLM	X

or

SMITH, HARRY	X

HE'S PROVED HIS WORTH

On election day you want the voter to put an "x" by your name when he or she is in the voting booth. Use the same ballot design on all literature accompanied by the campaign slogan.

The candidate should note that each factory has two or three shifts and up to four entrances for workers. This could easily entail ten to twelve individual visits to each large factory.

13. On election day, have someone drive the candidate to each polling division so the candidate can thank and encourage the workers. Then the candidate can relax in the evening and watch the results before giving a victory speech!

Index

Abbott, Doug 20
Act of Union 130
Aitken, Max (Lord Beaverbrook) 12
Alberta Heritage Trust Fund 162
Alliance Party. See Canadian Alliance
    Party
Aluminum Company of Canada 113
Andre, Harvie 102, 163
Anglo-Newfoundland Development
    Company 32-3
Asselin, Martial 58
Attlee, Clement 169
Avro Arrow 16, 30-1
Axworthy, Lloyd 72

Backbenchers 26
Baker, Walter 99
Balcer, Léon 18, 27, 55
Bank of Canada 16, 170, 190
Bélanger-Campeau Commission 125-6
Bell, Dick 69
Bennett, Bill 17
Bennett, W.A.C. 34
Benson, Edgar 176
Bertrand, Gabby 111-12
Bertrand, Jean-Jacques 75, 80
Bilingualism 51, 86
Bill 22, 143
Blaikie, Peter 101
Blais-Grenier, Suzanne 110
Bloc Québécois 12, 119, 125
Bomarc Missile Crisis 17, 57, 60, 62
Borden, Robert 12, 134-6
Bouchard, Lucien 111, 148
Boudria, Don 105
Bourassa, Robert 76, 111, 143, 146, 148-9
Bourbonnais, Marcel 42
British North America Act 21, 131
Brome-Missisquoi 18, 42, 51, 59, 62, 77,

    103, 106, 111, 116-7, 120, 180, 195
Brunet, Michel 128
Bryce, Bob 169

Cameron, Colin 57
Camp, Dalton 64, 66
Campbell, Kim 114-15
Canada Cement 12
Canada Mortgage and Housing 72-3
Canada-U.K. relations 51
Canada-U.S. relations 34, 37, 48-50, 54,
    60, 62
Canadian Alliance Party 12, 125, 164
Canadian dollar 16, 40, 169, 190
Canadian National Railway 51
Canadian Pacific Railway 152, 154-6
Canadian Tax Act 175
Caouette, Réal 35, 46, 52, 56, 173
Capital punishment 64
Carter, Kenneth 46
CCF Party 29, 156
Chamberlain, James 30
Charest Report 148
Charest, Jean 113, 115, 118-21
Charlottetown Accord 113-14
Charter of Rights and Freedoms 144-6
Chevrier, Lionel 36, 55
Chrétien, Jean 13-14, 26, 120, 122, 145,
    190, 192
Churchill, Gordon 46, 58, 173
Churchill, Sir Winston 60, 169
Cité Libre 64, 114, 140
Civil service 19-20, 63-4, 73, 166-79,
    185-6
Clark, Joe 12, 18, 29, 39, 74-5, 78, 82-
    102, 104-9, 120-124, 163, 173-4,
    181-2, 184, 192-3
Cogger, Michel 104, 107, 111-12
Columbia River Treaty 33-4

Common Market 47, 51
Commonwealth 47-8
Confederation 130-31, 133, 153-54
Confederation 22
Conscription 135-39
Constitutional Accord 1987 147-9
Constitutional Act 1982 145-6
Cournoyer, Louis 63, 106-8
Coyne Affair, The 22-5, 38, 166
Coyne, James 22-5, 179
Créditistes 35, 43, 52
Crosbie, John 97, 106, 174-6
Cross, James 142
Crow's Nest freight policy 124
Cuban Missile Crisis 48-51
Culver, David M. 113
Customs Union with U.S. 190
Dalton, Hugh 169
Davey, Keith 61
Davis, Bill 99
Day, Stockwell 18

Depression, The Great 158-9
Derrick, Brian 97
Diefenbaker, John 15-69, 96; becomes
    leader 18; character 25, 45-6;
    criticism of 39; political appoint-
    ments 27-8, 45; relations with media
    18-19, 36, 40, 62-3; relations with
    Quebec 18; relations with U.S. 34, 37;
    tactics 27
Diefenbaker, Olive 62
Diefendollars 41
Douglas, Tommy 19, 47, 61, 188
Drapeau, Jean 72, 138
Drew, George 15, 80, 89-90
Duplessis, Maurice 17, 79-80, 125, 137,
    139
Dupuis, Yvon 61
Durham's Report, Lord 126-7, 129-30,
    134

Education 190-1
Eisenhower, Dwight 34

Elections, Federal 58-63; (1957) 15;
    (1962) 16, 39-44; (1963) 27, 63, 120;
    (1968) 70; (1972) 80; (1979) 90-2
Environment 192

Faribeault, Marcel 69, 71
Favreau,Guy 64
Federal-provincial relations 34
Finance, Department of 20, 166-79
Fisher, Doug 170
Fleming, Donald 15-17, 20, 24, 27, 40,
    65, 166, 175
FLQ 142
Flynn, Jacques 44, 77
Foreign Investment Review Agency
    (FIRA) 163
Fraser, Al 188
Fraser, John 75, 82
Free Trade Agreement (FTA) 13, 156, 164
Frégault, Guy 128-29
Fulton, Davie 17, 33, 55, 65, 83

Gagné, Reine 68
Garneau, François-Xavier 127-8
Gélinas, Philippe 126
Gillies, James 87
Gillis, Roland 42
Glassco Royal Commission 47
Godbout, Adélard 79
Goods and Services Tax (GST) 13, 112-14
Gordon, Walter 38, 41, 43, 170-71, 175-6
Governor General 17
Green, Howard 43, 57

Halpenny, Ernest 58
Hamilton, Alvin 13, 57, 65
Hamilton, Bill 124
Harkness, Doug 48, 53
Harper, Stephen 164
Harris, Walter 166
Haultain, Frederick 153
Health care 186
Hees, George 27, 57, 65, 195
Hellyer, Paul 72-3, 82, 84, 87

Horner, Jack 82, 84-5
Houde, Mayor Camilien 138-9
Howe, C.D. 12
Hudon, Marc 43

Ignatieff, George 49
International Joint commission 33
International Union of Mines, Mill and
    Smelter Workers (Local 598) 42
International Woodworkers of America
    (IWA) 31-3
Iron Ore Company of Canada 100, 105

Johnson, Daniel 17, 65, 94, 146
Johnson, Pierre-Marc 146
Jones, Frank P. 12

Kennedy, John F. 34, 37, 51
Kerr, Tom 38
King, Mackenzie 17, 57, 71, 79, 137-9,
    185
Kingsley, Jean-Pierre 105
Kirby, Cam 82
Knowles, Stanley 174
Kolber, Leo 13

Lalonde, Marc 88-9
LaMarsh, Judy 36, 58, 61
Lambert, Marcel 48, 58
Lamontagne, Maurice 38
Landry, Bernard 119
Lane, Max 32
Lapointe, Ernest 71
LaSalle, Roch 90
Laurendeau, André 138
Laurier, Sir Wilfrid 17, 19, 133, 153
Lesage, Jean 34, 39, 50, 61, 94
Lévesque, René 70, 91, 141, 146
Lewis, David 44, 55
Liberal Party 12, 14, 17, 19, 36;
    policy 37-8, 40, 43, 58, 93, 118-20,
    122, 134, 146, 184
Liberal Party of Quebec 119, 137, 140
Lionel Groulx, Father 128

Lortie, Jean-Yves 102, 104
Loughheed, Peter 69, 82-3, 158, 161
Lowe, Frank 74

MacDonald, Flora 82-4, 87
Macdonald, Sir John A. 18-19, 57, 124,
    132, 153, 155
MacEachen, Allan 98, 174-8
Mackasey, Bryce 76
MacKay, Elmer 102
Mackenzie, Alexander 153
MacLennan, Hugh, 35
Macmillan, Harold 51, 60
Manitoba Red River Railway 154-5
Martin Sr., Paul 16, 171
Martin, Paul 122, 179, 190
Maudling, Reginald 47
Mazinkowski, Don 163
McCutcheon, Wallace 47, 55, 65
McGee, Frank 58
McKnight, Bill 102
McMurtry, Roy 145
McNaughton, General 34
Medicare 11, 64, 119, 184
Meech Lake Accord 113-14, 147-9
Meighen, Arthur 57, 138
Mercier, Honoré 133
Mercure, Gilles 111
Mireault, Gaëtan 63
Monteith, Waldo 57
Morgan, Keith 105
Morin, Claude 144
Mouvement des Caisses Populaires
    Desjardins 126
Mouvement souveraineté-association
    (MSA) 141-2
Mulroney, Brian 13, 29, 77, 82, 85-92,
    95-6, 99-102, 104-17, 120, 146, 148,
    163, 182

Nader, Ralph 26
National Energy Program 161-3
National Policy 153-5, 157, 164
National Resources Mobilization Act 138

Nationalism 35
Nationalization 141
NATO 51-2, 189
New Democratic Party (NDP) 44, 61-3, 97-8, 110, 170
Newfoundland 20-2; Term 29 20-2; Confederation 22
Newfoundland Brotherhood of Wood Workers 32
Newfoundland Loggers' Strike 17, 31-3
Nicholson, Commissioner L. H. 32
Nielsen, Eric 64
Night of the Long Knives 145
Norquay, John 154
Nowlan, George 46, 53, 55-6, 82, 170

October Crisis 142-3
Ouellet, André 145

Papineau, Louis-Joseph 129
Paradis, Denis 120
Paradis, Pierre 120
Paris, Anne 70
Parizeau, Jacques 118
Parliamentary committees 26-7
Parliamentary reform 186-8
Parti Québécois 142-4, 146
Patriotes 129
Patronage 94-5, 110
Pearkes, George 26
Pearson, Lester B. 15, 47-8, 50, 55, 60, 63-4, 74, 168, 172
Pellant, Luce 68
Pelletier, Gérard 91
Pelletier, Jean 73
Petro-Canada 96-7
Pickersgill, Jack 14, 20, 36
Pipeline Debate (1957) 15, 20
Pitfield, Michael 88-9
Political appointments 94-5, 112
Populism 35, 39 157
Poverty 190-1
Power Corporation 104
Price, General Basil 126-7

Prime Minister's Office (PMO) 19
Privatization 96-7
Privy Council 68, 173
Progressive Conservative Party 14, 18, 64-8, 157-8, 180-4, 192-3; candidate selection 123, 181; conventions 82-3, 86, 109; debt 180; delegate selection 18, 67, 102, 106-9, 182-3; grass roots 18, 119; leadership 64-8, 86, 114, 121, 182, 192-3; membership 180-3; party elections 18; Montreal office 18-19; situation in Quebec 39, 65-6, 75, 79-80, 89, 101, 119; policy 14, 40, 56, 59-60, 64, 69, 81; Western support 163

Quiet Revolution 34, 140-2

Rae, Bob 97
Rasminsky, Louis 25
Referendum (Quebec) 118, 144-7
Reform Party 164
Research and development 191
Ricard, Théogène 58, 76
Riel, Louis 132-34
Ritchie, Charles 48-9, 53, 60
Robertson, Brenda 181-2
Roblin, Duff 50, 65-6, 109
Romanow, Roy 145
Ryan, Claude 143

St-Laurent, Louis 15, 20, 71, 80, 166

Safety Sense Institute 73
Sauvé, Paul 68
Scott, Tom 132
Séguin, Maurice 128
Sévigny, Pierre 27, 58-9
Sharp, Mitchell 73, 168, 171
Shaw, Walter 50
Shawinigate 122
Sifton, Clifford 151
Smallwood, Joey 20-1, 32, 34, 50
Smith, Arthur 26
Social Credit (Alberta) 159

Social Credit Party (*See also*
Créditistes) 44, 54-7, 61
Speyer, Chris 102
St. Lawrence Seaway 55
Stamp Act (1765) 167-8
Stanfield, Robert 13, 29, 65-6, 68-83,
109, 171, 173
Starr, Michael 13, 35, 65
Stevens, Sinclair 82, 87-8

Taylor, Kenneth 170
Television 36, 93
Term 29 20-2
Tétrault, Jacques 104-5
Thompson, Robert 54-5, 61
Transfer payments 186
Treasury Board 173
Tremblay, Arthur 94
Trudeau, Michel 70
Trudeau, Pierre Elliott 12-13, 64, 68,
70-2, 74, 78, 81, 93-4, 96, 112, 138,
144, 161-2

Turner, John 112
Two Nations 69, 78

Union Nationale 17, 39, 75-6, 79-80,
137-40, 143
United Farmers Party 156

Vander Zalm, Bill 147
Vanier, Governor General Georges 48
Wage and price controls 81
Wagner, Claude 75-8, 82, 87, 91, 116,
120
War Measures Act 74
Wayne, Elsie 115
Weekend Magazine 74-5
Western immigration 150-2
Western regionalism 150-2
Winnipeg General Strike 33, 157
Winters, Robert 172
Wolf, Walter 104
World War I 134
World War II 71, 74, 158-60, 189